The Bible and Alcohol Use

Glen Striemer

All rights reserved. No part of this publication may be reproduced, distributed, or transmitted in any form or by any means, including photocopying, recording, or other electronic or mechanical methods, without the prior written permission of the publisher, except in the case of brief quotations embodied in critical reviews and certain other noncommercial uses permitted by copyright law. For permission requests, write to the publisher, TEACH Services, Inc., at the address below.

Copyright © 2020 Glen Striemer
Copyright © 2020 TEACH Services, Inc.
ISBN-13: 978-1-4796-1202-4 (Paperback)
ISBN-13: 978-1-4796-1203-1 (ePub)
Library of Congress Control Number: 2020902380

Any references to historical events, real people, or real places are used fictitiously. Names, characters, and places are products of the author's imagination.

All scripture quotations, unless otherwise indicated, are taken from the KING JAMES VERSION (KJV): KING JAMES VERSION, public domain.

Scripture quotations marked as NAS are taken from the NEW AMERICAN STANDARD (NAS): Scripture taken from the NEW AMERICAN STANDARD BIBLE®, copyright© 1960, 1962, 1963, 1968, 1971, 1972, 1973, 1975, 1977, 1995 by The Lockman Foundation. Used by permission.

Scripture quotations marked AMP are taken from the AMPLIFIED BIBLE (AMP): Scripture taken from the AMPLIFIED® BIBLE, Copyright © 1954, 1958, 1962, 1964, 1965, 1987 by the Lockman Foundation. Used by Permission. (www.Lockman.org).

Dedication

This book is dedicated to worldlings and Christians alike who have been duped into believing that Jesus sanctioned the moderate use of alcoholic spirits. Alcohol has been Satan's #1 tool to destroy men, nations, and kingdoms since the beginning of time. If even one soul repents and turns away from using fermented alcohol, then the writing of this book will not have been in vain.

Table of Contents

In the Beginning 7
Hebrew and Greek Words for Wine 12
After the Flood 14
The Patriarch Job 16
Melchizedek and Abram 17
Lot in Sodom 20
Low Standards 22
The Priesthood 25
Eli, the Priest 27
Rulers 28
    Nabal 28
    Belshazzar 28
    Alexander the Great 29
    King David 29
    King Solomon 30
    Queen Esther 33
    Prime Minister Daniel 34
    King Herod 34
The Prophets 36
    Amos 37
    Habakkuk 37
    Hosea 37
    Isaiah 37

- Jeremiah 38
- Joel 39
- Micah 39
- Moses 40
- Zechariah 40
- John the Revelator 40

Jesus 42

The Passover 45

The Nazarene Vow 48

New Hearts 53

Church Members 55

The World 58

The Alcohol Poem 62

Liquor Sellers 63

Temperance 65

Help the Tempted 67

Alcohol and Health 69
- Brain 70
- Bones 71
- Cancer 71
- Circulation 71
- Headaches 71
- Heart 72
- Liver 72
- Lungs 72
- Medications 72
- Nerves 73
- Reproduction 73
- Stomach 73
- Wounds 74

Summary 75

Bibliography 77

In the Beginning

"As man came forth from the hand of his Creator, he was of lofty stature and perfect symmetry. His countenance bore the ruddy tint of health and glowed with the light of life and joy."[1]

"And the Lord God took the man, and put him into the garden of Eden to dress it and to keep it" (Gen 2:15).

"In this garden were trees of every variety, many of them laden with fragrant and delicious fruit. There were lovely vines, growing upright, yet presenting a most graceful appearance, with their branches drooping under their load of tempting fruit of the richest and most varied hues. It was the work of Adam and Eve to train the branches of the vine to form bowers, thus making for themselves a dwelling from living trees covered with foliage and fruit."[2] "The blue heavens were its dome; the earth, with its delicate flowers and carpet of living green, was its floor; and the leafy branches of the goodly trees were its canopy. Its walls were hung with the most magnificent adorning—the handiwork of the great Master Artist."[3] "Eden bloomed on earth…. No taint of sin…marred the fair creation."[4] "The great Jehovah had laid the foundations of the earth; He had dressed the whole world in the garb of beauty and had filled it with things useful to man."[5] **"And God saw everything that he had made, and, behold it was very good"** (Gen. 1:31).

> *In this garden were trees of every variety, many of them laden with fragrant and delicious fruit of the richest and most varied hues*

"To dress and keep [this garden] was not wearisome, but pleasant and invigorating.... The Creator prepared no place for the stagnating practice of indolence."[6] "Their intellectual power was but little less than that of angels.... They held converse with leaf and flower and tree, gathering from each the secrets of its life.... On every leaf of the forest...God's name was written."[7] "The sinless pair wore no artificial garments; they were clothed with a covering of light and glory...."[8]

Eating fruit from "the tree of knowledge had been made a test of their obedience and love to God."[9] "There was but one prohibition in all the vast creation...." "[Angels] told Adam and Eve... Satan purposed to do them harm."[10] Satan chose to employ "as his medium the serpent."[11] "The serpent was then one of the wisest and most beautiful creatures on the earth. It had wings, and while flying through the air presented an appearance of dazzling brightness, having the color and brilliancy of burnished gold. Resting in the rich-laden branches of the forbidden tree and regaling itself with the delicious fruit, it was an object to arrest the attention and delight the eye of the beholder."[12]

Eve "soon found herself gazing with mingled curiosity and admiration upon the forbidden tree. The fruit was very beautiful, and she questioned herself why God had withheld it from them.... Instead of fleeing from the spot she lingered wonderingly to hear a serpent speak."[13] It said, **"...Ye** shall not surely die: for God doth know that in the day ye eat thereof, then your eyes shall be opened, and ye shall be as gods, knowing good and evil" (Gen. 3: 4–5). "The serpent plucked the fruit…and placed it in the hands of the half-reluctant Eve…. Perceiving no evil results from [touching the fruit, she] did eat…. "She seemed to feel a vivifying power, and imagined herself entering upon a higher state of existence…. And now, having herself transgressed, she became the agent of Satan in working the ruin of her husband."[14]

Adam's "love, gratitude, and loyalty to the Creator—all were overborne by love to Eve….He could not endure the thought of separation….He resolved to share her fate; if she must die, he would die with her…. He decided to brave the consequences. He seized the fruit and quickly ate."[15] "The robe of light which had enshrouded them, now disappeared,…[and the] air… seemed to chill the guilty pair."[16] Adam "endeavored to cast the blame upon his wife, and thus upon God Himself."[17] **"The woman whom thou gavest to be with me, she gave me of the tree, and I did eat"** (Gen. 3:12). Eve's response was also to lay blame: **"The serpent beguiled me, and I did eat"** (Gen. 3:13).

Announcement of the penalty for transgression was swift. The beautiful serpent, the jewel of all creatures, was relegated "to become the most groveling and detested of them all,"[18] lest he forever mock mankind flying overhead in superiority. Evolutionists claim the snake once had appendages, proving it once flew, but the Bible already said that it did until it was cursed. **"Upon thy belly shalt thou go, and dust shalt thou eat all the days of thy life"** (Gen. 3:14).

Satan's existence was prophesied to come to an end. **"I will put enmity between thee and the woman, and between thy seed and her seed; it shall bruise thy head, and thou shalt bruise his heel"** (Gen. 3:15).

After sinning, Eve received this message from the Lord: **"Thy desire shall be to thy husband, and he shall rule over thee"** (Gen. 3:16). Adam's new position would also serve as his protection: **"Cursed is the ground for thy sake; in sorrow shalt thou eat of it all the days of thy life; thorns also and thistles shall it bring forth to thee; …in the sweat of thy face shalt thou eat bread, till thou return unto the ground; for out of it wast thou taken: for dust thou art, and unto dust shalt thou return"** (Gen. 3:17–19).

Heavenly angels were hastily "commissioned to guard the tree of life [with] beams of light having the appearance of a glittering sword. [Lest sin be perpetually immortalized], none of the family of Adam were permitted to pass"[19] to continue to eat of the tree of eternal life. Adam and Eve, "in a state of conscious guilt"[20] for their disobedience, were instructed to leave the Garden of Eden. "In humility and unutterable sadness they bade farewell to their beautiful home and went forth to dwell upon the earth, where rested the curse of sin."[21] The Lord mercifully clothed them with garments of animal skin for warmth. "As they witnessed in drooping flower and falling leaf the first signs of decay, Adam and his companion mourned more deeply than men now mourn over their dead. The death of the frail, delicate flowers was indeed a cause of sorrow; but when the goodly trees cast off their leaves, the scene brought vividly to mind the stern fact that death is the portion of every living thing."[22]

"The Garden of Eden remained upon the earth long after man had become an outcast from its pleasant paths. The fallen race were long permitted to gaze upon the home of innocence… at the cherubim-guarded gate…. Hither came Adam and his sons to worship God, [renewing] their vows of obedience…. When the tide of iniquity overspread the world, [resulting in its] destruction by a flood of waters, the hand that had planted Eden withdraw it from the earth. But in the final restitution, when there shall be a '**a new heaven and a new earth**' (Rev. 21:1). [Eden] is to be restored more gloriously adorned than at the beginning."[23]

"Through unending ages the inhabitants of sinless worlds shall behold, in that garden of delight, a sample of the perfect work of God's creation, untouched by the curse of sin—a sample of what the whole earth would have become, had man but fulfilled the Creator's glorious plan."[24]

Proof that the antediluvian race prior to the flood had perverted God's original creation by turning the pure fruit of the vine into fermented spirits is verified by the fact that antediluvian lives mirrored those of drunkards—they were fierce, evil, and disrespectful scoffers, who were corrupt and immoral pleasure seekers, and were disobedient unto their own destruction. God was dealing with a world full of eight-hundred-year-old giant drunkards who were steeped in idol worship. "**Every imagination of the thoughts of his heart was only evil continually**" (Gen. 6:5). Jesus summed up the first stage of humanity simply: "**They did eat, they drank…**" (Luke 17:27). We can rest assured it was not the pure unfermented grape juice that this gluttonous generation drank. Alcohol helped mar humanity made in His image to the place where God finally decreed: "**I will destroy man whom I have created from the face of the earth; …for it repenteth me that I have made them**" (Gen. 6:7).

"As it was in the days of Noe, so shall it be also in the days of the Son of man" (Luke 17:26). The days spoken of by Jesus also refer to the state of man prior to His second coming. Nary can a movie be made or a book be written by the secular mind in which a bottle of liquor is not prominently displayed in someone's hand. Not a sports game or a good time can seemingly be had without the blessing of the insidious liquor industry that is devoted to destroying men's lives.

Hebrew and Greek Words for Wine

The Dictionary Reference[25] defines *wine* as being:

1. an alcoholic drink produced from fruits and flowers fermented with water and sugar.
2. an intoxicating, cheering, or invigorating effect.
3. **fermented** grape juice containing an alcohol content of 14% or less together, with ethers and esters that give it bouquet and flavor.
4. **unfermented** juice of various fruits or plants.

The strong English inference is that wine is a fermented alcoholic beverage most of the time, but this interpretation leaves the door open, in rare cases, for it being unfermented wine. But, when we read an English translation of the Bible, only one word— *wine*—appears for all circumstances.

However, in the ancient Hebrew Bible, the use of the word *wine* suggests many different meanings. Here are the many different words (and their meanings) that were used in the Old Testament and New Testament.[26]

Hebrew (Old Testament)

Aciyc	Freshly squeezed juice; new, just-trodden sweet wine
Chamar	To ferment with scum; to glow with redness; trouble
Chemar	Wine as fermenting; pure, red wine
Cobe	A drink, especially an alcoholic beverage; drinking party; carousal; drunken; tipsy
Enab	To bear fruit; grape, ripe grape
Khehmed	Delight; desirable, pleasant

Mamcak	Wine mixture, as with water, spices; drink offering
Shathah	Imbibe; drunk
Shekar	Intoxicant; intensely alcoholic liquor; strong drink; drunkard
Tiyrosh	Expulsion of fresh grape juice; freshly squeezed new sweet wine; rarely fermented
Yayin	To give off bubbles of gas, as in fermenting liquors (effervesce); intoxication, banqueting, winebibber; rare reference to unfermented wine

Greek (New Testament)

Aparche	A product of the earth in its natural state (unfermented)
Glenkos	Sweet wine; fresh juice; also highly inebriating fermented wine
Gleukos	Sweet juice pressed from the grape; sweet wine
Killayown	Consumption; falling; destruction; pining
Oinos	Wine, literally or figuratively
Paroinos	Given to wine; drunken

After the Flood

However long it took for Noah to plant a vineyard and then wait for its harvest after the flood is open to speculation. What isn't questioned is what Noah did with the first harvest of grapes. Perhaps it was witnessing the devastation caused by the flood resulting in a landscape that barely resembled the earth he once knew—perhaps that weakened his resolve to remain faithfully pure. "Everywhere were strewn the dead bodies of men and beasts."[27] The turbid seas were blown by violent winds that shifted to cover their remains. A world that formerly knew no rain was now mostly covered in water. "The earth presented an appearance of confusion and desolation impossible to describe. The mountains, once so beautiful in their perfect symmetry, had become [jagged] and irregular."[28] Temperatures were now extreme compared to the terrarium-style existence enjoyed prior to the flood. The earth itself was now tilted, exposing the frigid barrenness of the north and south poles. Among the buried remains were fermenting forests and massive decay; this created extensive coal beds that mixed with lime and water, frequently igniting and resulting in earthquakes and volcanic eruptions above its surface. These natural phenomenons were God's chosen agents to alert the inhabitants that the end of this earth is inevitable.

Perhaps the immense responsibility resting upon the shoulders of the last patriarch of the antediluvian age was too much for him to bear, as Noah **"became heir of the righteousness which is by faith"** (Heb. 11:7), having received this responsibility that passed from Adam to Enoch and then to Methuselah; but Noah succumbed to the temptations of the antediluvian race by dulling his senses to reality through the use of fermented spirits.

"And Noah began to be an husbandman, and he planted a vineyard: And he drank of the wine [*yayin***—fermented], and was drunken…"** (Gen. 9:20–21).

One could say that Noah discovered the art of winemaking after harvesting the vineyard, but chances are more likely that the patriarch had enjoyed a drink or two prior to the flood, which would have been more in harmony with the social norms of the dark antediluvians. Thus, Noah is the first recorded drunkard in Scripture by name. The world would have been a better place had Noah discontinued the intricate art of winemaking this side of the flood. As so often is the case whenever alcohol is involved, shame and embarrassment closely followed: **"…And he was uncovered within his tent. And Ham, the father of Canaan, saw the nakedness of his father, and told his two brethren without. And Shem and Japheth took a garment, and laid it upon both their shoulders, and went backward, and covered the nakedness of their father …"** (Gen. 9:21–23).

The Patriarch Job

In the oldest recorded book of the Bible, the patriarch Job was so concerned over his sons' feasting with wine that he made sacrifices for them continually. **"His sons went and feasted in their houses, every one his day; and sent and called for their three sisters to eat and to drink with them. And it was so, when the days of their feasting were gone about, that Job sent and sanctified them, and rose up early in the morning, and offered burnt offerings according to the number of them all: for Job said, It may be that my sons have sinned, and cursed God in their hearts. Thus did Job continually"** (Job 1:4–5).

And so it has ever been the pattern of concerned parents to fret over the wayfaring ways of their children who are involved with alcohol. They offer intercessory prayer when their reasoning and pleadings are ignored. Deep down inside, parents know that cursing God and alcohol go hand in hand. Satan was very present in this case, and nothing has changed, as he continually seeks the destruction of our loved ones with alcohol—his favorite medium.

"And there was a day when his sons and his daughters were eating and drinking wine [*yayin*—fermented] in their eldest brother's house" (Job 1:13). Satan's fury was unleashed without reserve, and a servant carried the sad news to their father Job: **"Thy sons and thy daughters were eating and drinking wine [*yayin*] in their eldest brother's house: and, behold, there came a great wind from the wilderness, and smote the four corners of the house, and it fell upon the young men, and they are dead…"** (Job 1:18–19).

Every circumstance differs, but how many God-fearing parents have lost their precious offspring when one common denominator was present—alcohol—which numbs the senses and invites the devil's wrath.

Melchizedek and Abram

The king of Elam and allies had invaded Sodom and Gomorrah, and, among those taken captive, were Abram's nephew Lot and his family. Abram organized a small army and surprised the victorious Elamites, who had given themselves up to reveling, and this resulted in their utter destruction. Abram turned down the opportunity to claim the spoils of rich booty and subsequent indebtedness to the king of Sodom, saying, **"I will not take from a thread even to a shoelatchet…lest thou shouldest say, I have made Abram rich"** (Gen. 14:23).

As a type of Christ, Melchizedek, king of Salem (the city which would eventually become Jerusalem) came forth: **"And Melchizedek, king of Salem, brought forth bread and wine [***yayin***—fermented]: and he was the priest of the most high God. And he… said, blessed be Abram…"** (Gen. 14:18–19). Abram responded by paying tithes to the king. Later, in the seventh chapter of the book of Hebrews, Paul used this story to illustrate how Abraham's offspring Levi paid tithes to the priestly order of Melchizedek while he was still in his father's loins. Melchizedek had no beginning or end of his priestly lineage. The same is true of Jesus; thus proving that Jesus was qualified to be Israel's heavenly High Priest because He, too, was of the unending priesthood of Melchizedek, who was superior to Abram (the father of the Levitical priesthood), even though He, Jesus, was from the tribe of Judah.

As a type of Christ, brought forth bread and wine, this event was also a forerunner of the communion service of the Last Supper

This event was also a forerunner of the communion service of the Last Supper, where bread and wine were brought forth. The word used for *wine* in Melchizedek's bread and wine is *yayin*— a rare reference to unfermented wine. It is our conclusion that this was the rare instance, due to the direct implications that pointed forward to our Savior, whose sinless life on earth was typified by unleavened bread and unfermented wine.

God used the life of Abraham to define the two Covenants. At his best, Abraham typified all that was well in the New Covenant experience: **"He believed in the Lord; and he counted it to him for righteousness"** (Gen. 15:6). Nowhere in the gospel does salvation get any simpler or purer than this declaration.

At his worst, Abraham typified Old Testament living, which was rife with polygamy, divorce, slavery, prostitution, an eye-for-an-eye mentality, murder, and stoning sinners. As difficult as it is for modern Christians to understand, the Israelite lifestyle was conservative compared to that of the undisciplined and ungodly heathen nations surrounding them.

Drinking alcohol became a way of life for God's chosen people. Winepresses abounded, and often the primary goal of Israel appeared to be the harvest of a good crop of grapes for winemaking. God's people resorted to drinking mixed wines and strong drink to ease the burden of life. There appears to have been no abstainers among the patriarchs, other than those who took a vow of abstinence or were in mourning. In the many situations in Scripture where fermented alcohol was involved, rarely was there a positive result.

It is a sad realization that unfermented wine was available to the ancient Jews, but some continually chose the fermented. Ancient civilizations had several says of preventing fruit juices from fermenting, so that they were able to have nonalcoholic wine (grape juice) throughout the year. One method involved boiling the juice and reducing it to a syrup that could later be diluted with water. Another method was to boil the juice with minimal evaporation and then immediately seal it in airtight jars with beeswax. Also, drying the fruit in the sun and reconstituting it with water was used, adding sulphur to the fruit juice. Filtering the juice to extract the gluten was also a method that would prevent fermentation. The ancients would also boil fermented wine to eliminate alcohol. The poet Horace (65 B.C.) wrote that the wine of Lesbos was sweet, like nectar, and would not produce intoxication.[29] The Mishna (a collection of oral Jewish traditions) states that the Jews were in the habit of drinking boiled wine.[30] In his commentary on the gospel of John, Albert Barnes wrote, "The wine of Judea was the pure juice of the grape without any mixture of alcohol."[31]

Adam Clarke wrote, "Wine anciently, was the mere expressed juice of the grape without fermentation."[32]

Unsanctified living was never God's final plan. Hard-hearted Old Covenant followers were tolerant of alcohol use and many other sins. Old Covenant lifestyles were not time-sensitive, divided neatly by the Cross. Unfortunately, there are legions of similar believers wandering around today, with bottle in hand, and with much sin resulting. **"But where sin abounded, grace did much more abound ... What shall we say then? Shall we continue in sin, that grace may abound? God forbid..."** (Rom. 5:20; 6:1–2).

Lot in Sodom

Lot's peril was due to his selfishness in formerly choosing the best land for himself when he **"...pitched his tent toward Sodom"** (Gen. 13:12). Rescued once from his experience in Sodom, Lot returns to the most sinful city in the world. Like so many modern cities, Sodom was rife with "mirth and revelry, feasting and drunkenness. The vilest and most brutal passions were unrestrained."[33] "The inhabitants of Sodom had passed the limits of divine forbearance...and the fires of [God's] vengeance were about to be kindled in the vale of Siddim."[34]

Jesus summed up the fate of Sodom with those who perished in the flood in these few words, **"Likewise also as it was in the days of Lot; they did eat, they drank..."** (Luke 17:28). Men marvel at the immorality flaunted in today's society. Look no further than the influence of alcoholic beverages. They lower men's morals to less than those of brute beasts. The end result of the sinful Sodomites parallels that class of wine bibbers living in our day who are oblivious to the signs of the times all around them.

"...it rained fire and brimstone from heaven, and destroyed them all. Even thus shall it be in the day when the Son of man is revealed" (Luke 17: 29–30). **"And Lot went up out of Zoar, and dwelt in the mountain, and his two daughters with him.... And the firstborn said unto the younger, Our father is old, and there is not a man in the earth to come in unto us after the manner of all the earth: Come, let us make our father drink wine** [*yayin*—fermented]**, and we will lie with him, that we may preserve seed of our father"** (Gen. 19:30–38).

In the days of Abraham's nephew Lot, alcohol was so common that his daughters simply had to persuade their father to drink existing wine stocks. How drunk must Lot have been to not recognize his own daughters (we give him the benefit of the doubt), throw all decency to the wind, and engage in these immoral acts? Descendants of the two sons born through this debauchery formed two nations, the Moabites and the Ammonites, who later became the bitterest enemies of the Hebrew race.

Low Standards

The Jews turned to wine and strong drink for happiness. **"And if the way be too long for thee, so that thou art not able to carry it** [tithe of the increase of seed]**...Then shalt thou turn it** [tithe] **into money...And thou shalt bestow that money for whatsoever thy soul lusteth after...for wine** [*yayin*—fermented]**, or for strong drink** [*shekar*—intoxicant; intensely alcoholic liquor; strong drink]**, or for whatsoever thy soul desireth: ...and thou shalt rejoice, thou, and thine household..."** (Deut. 14:24–26). This counsel to purchase strong drink, that their souls lusted after, is along the lines of God allowing situations such as polygamy, divorce, and slavery. Low were the patriarchs' standards when compared with those of New Testament believers and Christians today.

"**...The spoiler is fallen upon thy summer fruits and upon thy vintage... and I have caused wine** [*yayin*—fermented] **to fail from the winepresses: none shall tread with shouting; their shouting shall be no shouting**" (Jer. 48:32–33). It is hard to imagine any situation today—short of someone winning the lottery—where shouting for joy is the norm. But such was the reward for harvesting the pure fruit and the making of fermented wine. Hard punishment to the Old Covenant hearts was the taking away of their wine. It was like taking a pacifier away from a baby, candy from a child, or the bottle from the drunkard. Be certain that a rebellion will ensue.

"**The Lord of hosts shall defend them; ...and they shall drink** [*shathah*—imbibe; drunk] **and make a noise as through wine** [*yayin*—fermented].... **And the Lord their God shall save them in that day as the flock of his people...**" (Zech. 9:15–16). If anyone doubts the mercy of God in the Old Testament, look no further than this verse, which demonstrates God's willingness to save a murderous, idolatrous, nation often prone to alcohol abuse. Once saved by grace, it was then God's plan to sanctify this people.

Buying and selling wine had become vital to the Jewish economy. **"Judah, and the land of Israel, they were thy merchants: they traded in thy market…. Damascus was thy merchant in the multitude of the wares of thy making, for the multitude of all riches; in the wine** [*yayin*—fermented] **of Helbon, and white wool"** (Ezek. 27:17–18).

"Forasmuch therefore as your treading is upon the poor, …ye have planted pleasant vineyards, but ye shall not drink wine [*yayin*—fermented] **of them"** (Amos 5:11). Those who oppress the poor shall not reap the joy of drinking wine. Symbolically, the Jews were given many Scripture passages that pointed forward to their Messiah, but, when He came, they rejected Him and His Father, the Husbandman of the vineyard.

Examine these Old Testament suggestions for alcohol consumption, as outlined in Proverbs 31, verses 6–7:

1. **"Give strong drink** [*shekar*—intoxicant; intensely alcoholic liquor] **unto him that is ready to perish"** (Prov. 31:6), meaning a person who is on his or her deathbed without hope in the resurrection. This was in harmony with the practice of mercifully giving stupefying drink to those criminals in great pain who were being crucified. It is worth noting, however, that Jesus refused the influence of wine to lessen His pain. **"They gave Him to**

drink wine [*oinos*—wine, literally or figuratively] **mingled with myrrh: but He received it not"** (Mark 15:23).

2. **"[Give] wine** [*yayin*—fermented] **unto those that be of heavy hearts"** (Prov. 31:6), meaning those who are depressed or in mourning. The KJV Bible marginal note on this verse suggests that *heavy hearts* are those that are *bitter of soul.*

3. **"Let him drink** [*shathah*—imbibe; drunk]**, and forget his poverty,"** meaning those who are poor but do not trust in God's promises to deliver them from temporal want.

4. **"And remember his misery no more,"** meaning those who are in misery from physical, emotional, spiritual, or temporal wants. Fermented drink was for those who were temporarily weak in mind, body, or spirit.

The Priesthood

The priesthood was set apart to be holy, as defined in great detail in the books of Moses. The apostles would later use these illustrations to prove that Christians are a peculiar people, set apart for holy living. They would be followers of Jesus, living in this world, but not of it.

"**And the Lord spake unto Aaron, saying, Do not drink wine** [*yayin*—fermented] **nor strong drink** [*shekar*—intoxicant/ intensely alcoholic liquor; strong drink], **thou, nor thy sons with thee, when ye go into the tabernacle of the congregation…that ye may put difference between holy and unholy, and between unclean and clean**" (Lev. 10:8–10). In the face of wide spread alcohol use, God placed restrictions on the holy priesthood, setting them apart from the common people, so that they would be able to discern His will. "**Neither shall any priest drink wine** [*yayin*—fermented], **when they enter into the inner court**" (Ezek. 44:21). "**And this shall be the priest's due from the people, from them that offer a sacrifice, whether it be ox or sheep… the firstfruit also…of thy wine** [*tiyrosh*—expulsion of fresh grape juice; freshly squeezed new sweet wine]…" (Deut. 18:3–4). Worshippers brought the first fruits of unfermented wine to the priests, not the fermented by-product of the grape.

> *Worshippers brought the first fruits of unfermented wine to the priests, not the fermented by-product of the grape*

Strangely, we do find an instance in which fermented wine was used in the sanctuary services: "**…and the fourth part of an hin of wine** [*yayin*—*fermented*] **for a drink offering**" (Exod. 29:40). Fermentation is likened in the Bible to sin, as in the leavened bread versus the unleavened. We need look no further than this verse as to why God would order fermented spirits to be used in the holy services: "**For he hath made him to be sin for us, who knew no sin; that**

we might be made the righteousness of God in him" (2 Cor. 5:21). Christ "suffered the death which was ours, that we might receive the life which was His. 'With His stripes we are healed.'"[35]

Eli, the Priest

"Now Hannah, she spake in her heart; only her lips moved, but her voice was not heard: therefore Eli thought she had been drunken. And Eli said unto her, *"How long wilt thou be drunken? Put away thy wine* [yayin—fermented] *from thee* [italics supplied]. **And Hannah answered and said,** *"No, my lord…I have drunk neither wine* [yayin] *nor strong drink"* [shekar—intoxicant; intensely alcoholic liquor] [italics supplied] (1 Sam. 1:13-15). Eli, the priest, wrongfully accused Hannah of drinking fermented beverages, referencing something that seemed quite familiar to them both. Hannah's response shows how common and widespread drinking alcohol was in ancient Israel, even among the women.

Rulers

Nabal

"Now the name of the man was Nabal; …[he] was churlish and evil in his doings" (1 Sam. 25:3). **And Abigail came to Nabal; and, behold, he held a feast in his house, like the feast of a king; and Nabal's heart was merry within him, for he was very drunken"** (1 Sam. 25:36). We clearly see that the feasts of kings were steeped in drunkenness. Nabal was hung over from drinking, when a heart attack suddenly ended his life (1 Sam. 25:37).

Belshazzar

"Belshazzar the king made a great feast to a thousand of his lords, and drank wine [*chamar*—to ferment with scum; to glow with redness; trouble] **before the thousand. Belshazzar, whiles he tasted the wine** [*chamar*], **commanded to bring the golden and silver vessels which his father Nebuchadnezzar had taken out of the temple which was in Jerusalem; that the king, and his princes, his wives, and his concubines, might drink therein…. They drank wine**[*chamar*], **and praised the gods of gold, and of silver, of brass, of iron, of wood, and of stone. In that same hour came forth fingers of a man's hand, and wrote over against the candlestick upon the plaister of the wall of the king's palace…. Then was Daniel brought in before the king…This is the interpretation of the thing: MENE; God hath numbered thy kingdom and finished it. TEKEL; Thou art weighed in the balances and found wanting. PERES; Thy kingdom is divided, and given to the Medes and Persians….In that night was Belshazzar the king of the Chaldeans slain. And Darius the Median took the kingdom…"** (Daniel 5:1–2, 4–5, 13, 26–28, 30–31).

Thus ended the reign of Babylon, the first of four kingdoms prophesied to rule the world (Dan. 2:37-40). Alcohol was a key factor in its overthrow. As there was a heavenly Witness at the feast of Babylon, there is also a

Witness in every scene of sacrilegious mirth, recording the names of those who are being weighed in the balances of eternity.

Alexander the Great

The third prophesied world kingdom was Greece. Even though the Grecian armies were symbolized by the speed of the leopard, their leader, Alexander the Great, could not outrun the ravages of alcohol abuse. This emperor died in his early thirties in a drunken stupor before he could enjoy the spoils of his global rule. Alexander conquered the world, but, in the end, alcohol conquered him. "[Alexander] is said to have wept that he had not another world to conquer. For what? That he might do good to his fellow-men, bless and elevate the race…? No— but to gratify his own insatiable thirst for power, and to pander to his ungovernable lusts. With contemptible arrogance, he claimed for himself divine honors…. He himself often murdered his own friends and favorites in his drunken frenzies…. He encouraged such excessive drinking among his followers that on one occasion twenty of them together died as the result of their carousal. At length, having sat through one long drinking spree, he was immediately invited to another, when, after drinking to each of the twenty guests present, he twice drank full, says history, …the Herculean cup containing six of our quarts. He thereupon fell down, seized with a violent fever, of which he died eleven days later [in the very prime of life]."[36]

"Such was Alexander, whom the fulsome pages of history style the 'Great.' If vice, and cruelty, and vainglory, and love of power, and thirst for blood, constitute greatness, he was great; if otherwise, he was a monster… because his powers of mind, some of which he possessed to a remarkable degree, were prostituted to unholy ends."[37]

King David

It is wondered how the shepherd boy, a man after God's own heart, could commit adultery and murder, and then lust after wives and concubines. The following verses establish David's pattern of drinking fermented spirits, which was devilishly designed to loosen any man's morals. "**…The servant of Mephibosheth met him…with a bottle of wine** [*yayin*— fermented]…**that such as be faint in the wilderness may drink**" (2 Sam. 16:1–2). "**And** [David] **dealt…the whole multitude of Israel…bread, and a good piece of flesh, and a flagon of wine**" [*yayin*] (2 Sam. 6:19). By the time of David's ascent to the throne, wine and feasting were an established way of life for most of the chosen nation. "**…And all the rest of Israel** were of one heart to make David king. And there they were with David three days, eating and drinking..." [*shathah*—imbibe, drunk] (1 Chron. 12:38–39). "And over the king's treasures was Azmaveth...and over the vineyards was Shimei...: over the increase of the vineyards for the wine [*yayin*]cellars was Zabdi..." (1 Chron. 27:25–27). David was king over the world-class wine cellars at Jerusalem. "[That He may bring forth] wine [*yayin*] that maketh glad the heart of man" (Ps. 104:14–15).

Anyone who has ever witnessed a drunken man awake in a rage knows how fearful a sight this can be. **"For in the hand of the Lord there is a cup, and the wine [*yayin*—fermented] is red;** [*chamar*—to ferment with scum; to glow with redness; trouble] **it is full of mixture; and he poureth out of the same: but the dregs thereof, all the wicked of the earth shall wring them out, and drink them"** (Ps. 75:8). **"Thou hast shewed thy people hard things: thou hast made us to drink the wine (*yayin*) of astonishment"** (Ps. 60:3). The same verse in the New American Standard (NAS) version reads, **"You have given us wine to drink that makes us stagger"** (Ps. 60:3, NAS). **"Then the Lord awaked as one out of sleep, and like a mighty man that shouteth by reason of wine [*yayin*]"** (Ps 78:65).

Like father, like son. David's offspring continued in his alcohol-abusing and often sinful footsteps. **"Now Absalom had commanded his servants, saying, "Mark ye now when Ammon's heart is merry with wine, [*yayin*—fermented] and when I say unto you, Smite Ammon; then kill him..."** (2 Sam. 13:28). Ammon, the brother of Absalom, was obviously a pattern drinker of fermented wine. Ammon's vulnerability through drunkenness preceded his jealous murder by his own brother.

King Solomon

Solomon's reign was stained with the use of spirits. Alcohol abuse peaked during the apostasy of Solomon. Under his leadership, seeds were planted for the eventual breakup of the kingdom of Israel, from which it never recovered. How much alcohol was a factor in Israel's demise we can only speculate, but there can be no doubt that the extravagant lifestyle of the world's wealthiest king was steeped in alcohol. In the building of the temple, Solomon poured out his generosity through wine: **"And behold, I will give to thy servants, the hewers that cut timber..., twenty thousand baths of wine [*yayin*—fermented]"** (2 Chron. 2:10).

The Bible book, *Song Of Solomon*, apparently written for one of Solomon's beloved wives, is interpreted as the picture of pure love, an allegory of the relation between Christ and His church. In Solomon's poetic verse he continually uses the word *wine* as an illustration to show his love. **"…thy love is better than wine [*yayin*—fermented]"** (Song of Sol. 1:2).

"The vines with the tender grape give a good smell" (Song of Sol. 2:13). **"…how much better is thy love than wine [*yayin*—fermented]!"** (Song of Sol. 4:10]. **"…we will remember thy love more than wine [*yayin*]…"** (Song of Sol. 1:4). **"…I have drunk my wine [*yayin*] with my milk…"** (Song of Sol. 5:1). **"The roof of thy mouth like the best wine [*yayin*] for my beloved, that goeth down sweetly, causing the lips of those that are asleep to speak"** (Song of Sol. 7:9). Reference is made to those who talk in their sleep after drinking what is termed the *best (or most potent) wine.* **"Let us get up early to the vineyards; let us see if the vine flourish, whether the tender grape appear"** (Song of Sol. 7:12). **"…I would cause thee to drink of spiced wine [*yayin*] of the juice of my pomegranate"** (Song of Sol. 8:2). Alcohol might explain how the wisest man could end up running after heathen women and watching as children were sacrificed to false gods.

Solomon's words in the book of Ecclesiastes pitifully describe the experience of the drunkard: **"I said in mine heart, Go to now, I will prove thee with mirth, therefore enjoy pleasure: and, behold, this also is vanity…. I sought in mine heart to give myself unto wine [*yayin*—fermented]… I planted me vineyards…And whatsoever mine eyes desired I kept not from them…. I hated life."** (Eccles. 2:1, 3, 4, 10,17). King Solomon may have hated life, but, during this period, he did not hate what was one of the main

causes of his miserable condition: "**...Drink thy wine [*yayin*] with a merry heart**" (Eccles. 9:7). "**Wine [*yayin*] makes life merry**" (Eccles. 10:19, NAS).

There can be no doubt that Solomon's reign was only a shadow of what it could have been. There was a decided shortage of spirituality during his kingship, but there was no shortage of alcoholic spirits. However, before he died, Solomon became the first of the Bible writers to counsel believers against the use of spirits, pointing out its various evils. The king finally spoke vigorously against the use of fermented spirits: "**Who hath woe? Who hath sorrow? Who hath contentions? Who hath babbling? Who hath wounds without cause? Who hath redness of eyes? They that tarry long at the wine [*yayin*—fermented]; they that go to seek mixed wine [*mamcak*—**wine mixture, as with water, spices; drink offering]" (Prov. 23:29–30). "**Wine [*yayin*] is a mocker, strong drink [*shekar*—intoxicant; intensely alcoholic liquor] is raging: and whosoever is deceived thereby is not wise**" (Prov. 20:1). "**Look not thou upon the wine [*yayin*] when it is red, when it giveth his colour in the cup, when it moveth itself aright. At the last it biteth like a serpent, and stingeth like an adder**" (Prov. 23:31–32). "**...He that loveth wine [*yayin*] and oil shall not be rich**" (Prov. 21:17). "**Be not among the winebibbers...for the drunkard...shall come to poverty**" (Prov. 23:20–21). "**Enter not into the path of the wicked avoid it, pass not by it, turn from it...for they...drink the wine [*yayin*] of violence**" (Prov. 4:14, 17).

It was eventually recommended by Solomon that those in political leadership should abstain from spirits, undoubtedly recounting his own errors: "**It is not for kings to drink wine [*yayin*—fermented]; nor for princes strong drink [*shekar*—intoxicant; intensely alcoholic liquor; strong drink]: lest they drink, and forget the law, and pervert the judgment of any of the afflicted**" (Prov. 31:4, 5). "**Wisdom...hath mingled her wine [*yayin*]..., come drink of the wine [*yayin*] which I have mingled** (Prov. 9:1, 5). Israel knew all too well the effects of being drunk. Symbolically, Solomon states that wisdom from God is portrayed as something a man should be drunk with, not alcohol. Thanks to Solomon's eventual strict stand against alcohol, Christians can live today in happy sobriety. New Testament writers emphasizing holy living used the wise man's counsel to instruct new believers.

The sin of alcohol use continued to pass through generations of David's offspring, always with predictable results: "**Rehoboam... fortified the strong holds, and put captains in them, and store of victual, and of oil and wine**" [*yayin*—fermented] (2 Chron. 11:1, 11] "**...I the Lord thy God am a jealous God, visiting the iniquity of the fathers upon the children** unto the third and fourth generation of them that hate me; and shewing mercy unto thousands of them that love me and keep my commandments" (Exod. 20:5–6).

Queen Esther

"Now it came to pass in the days of Ahasuerus…the king made a feast…. And they gave them drink in vessels of gold…, and royal wine [*yayin*— fermented] in abundance…and the drinking was according to the law… for so the king had appointed to all the officers of his house, that they should do according to every man's pleasure….On the seventh day, when the heart of the king was merry with wine [*yayin*], he commanded…to bring Vashti the queen before the king with the crown royal, to shew the people and the princes her beauty….But the queen Vashti refused to come at the king's commandment:…therefore was the king very wroth, and his anger burned in him"** (Esther 1:1, 7–8, 10–12)…. It is likely that Vashti refused to appear because she would have been humiliated in some way. The king and his men had been feasting and drinking for seven days. It is almost assured that they did not have noble intentions in calling her to the party. While nothing specific is noted, the context—especially the reference to her beauty—indicates that her attendance at the feast was sought to entertain the men in some way.[38] **"[And the king's advisor said] if it please the king, let there go a royal commandment from him…that Vashti come no more before king Ahasuerus; and let the king give her royal estate unto another that is better than she"** (Esther 1:19). And that is how Esther became the queen.

Esther owed her rule as the new queen, in part, to the king's weakness for excessive drinking. Fortunately, there will always be followers of God who are temporate, as there is no record of Queen Esther using alcohol; but the Bible depicts how she used fermented spirits to her advantage. Brave Queen Esther knew the heart of her heathen husband could be loosed through wine, as a way to achieve the saving of Israel. **"And the king said unto Esther at the banquet of wine [*yayin*—fermented], What is thy petition? And it shall be granted thee: and what is thy request? Even to the half of the kingdom it shall be performed"** (Esther 5:6). How did Esther know the will of her heathen husband king? His extravagant feast-making and wine-drinking past was well documented for all to see, and she knew she could please him by making a feast in his honor. During the feast, she made a request of the king—a request that saved God's people from impending destruction.

Prime Minister Daniel

As a young man, Daniel, of the royal line, was taken captive by Babylon and fell under the commands of King Nebuchadnezzar. **"And the king appointed them a daily provision of...the wine [yayin—fermented] which he [the king] drank...But Daniel purposed in his heart that he would not defile himself with...the wine [yayin] which [the king] drank....Then said Daniel...let them give us...water to drink"** (Daniel 1:5, 8, 12). Daniel's stand for abstinence is historical and part of the reason why God gave him understanding in all visions and dreams. It is also why Nebuchadnezzar declared of Daniel and his friends: **"And in all matters of wisdom and understanding, that the king enquired of them, he found them ten times better than all the magicians and astrologers that were in his realm"** (Daniel 1:20).

Afterward, Daniel understood the 70-week prophecy, outlining the Messiah who was to come and Christ's prophesied rejection by the chosen nation (Dan. 9:24–26); this understanding caused Daniel to go into mourning: **"I ate no pleasant bread, neither came flesh nor wine [yayin—fermented] in my mouth, neither did I anoint myself at all, till three whole weeks were fulfilled"** (Dan. 10:3). This fast indicates that Daniel, the beloved, who was trained faithfully through childhood and then, as a young adult was able to withstand the king's temptations, may have taken the Nazarene vow of separation. This vow, included, among other things, that **"he shall separate himself from wine [yayin—fermented] and strong drink [shekar—intoxicant; intensely alcoholic liquor; strong drink], and shall drink no vinegar of wine [yayin], or vinegar of strong drink [shekar], neither shall he drink any liquor of grapes..."** (Numbers 6:3). There is a strong probability that exemplary Daniel never drank fermented spirits as, on rare occasions, the Hebrew word *yayin* can be translated as "unfermented."

King Herod

The Bible portrayal of the death of John the Baptist is brief (Matt. 14:1–12). However, one Bible commentary portrays the scene as it undoubtedly was. "On the king's birthday an entertainment was to be given to the officers of state and nobles of the court. There would be feasting and drunkenness. Herod would thus be thrown off his guard, and might then be influenced according to [Herodias'] will."[39] "The king was dazed with wine. Passion held sway, and reason was dethroned."[40] **"...The daughter of Herodias danced before them, and pleased Herod. Whereupon he**

promised with an oath to give her whatsoever she would ask. And she, being before instructed of her mother, said, Give me here John Baptist's head in a charger" (Matt. 14:6–8).

"The oath had been made in honor of his guests, and if one of them had offered a word against the fulfillment of his promise, he would gladly have spared the prophet.... But though shocked at the girl's demand, they were too besotted to interpose a remonstrance.... They had given themselves up to feasting and drunkenness until the senses were benumbed."[41]

The Prophets

God put the illustration of alcohol and its debilitating, addictive effects to marvelous use. After centuries of alcohol abuse, God uses alcohol as an object lesson to paint a description of a rebellious and stiff-necked people who had grown weak and dependent upon this substance.

He spoke to the people in language they knew all too well, through a substance they loved far too much. After Solomon's much-needed counsel against drinking (Prov. 20:1; Prov. 23:20–21, 29–32), God's prophets began to speak boldly concerning alcohol use among His beloved children. Drinking mixed spirits was prophetically symbolized as being a curse combined with the pending overthrow of their nation (as described in later sections). One must look long and hard to find any prophetic passage where drinking alcohol is symbolically blessed.

Amos

"...They drink the wine [*yayin*—fermented] of the condemned in the house of their god" (Amos 2:8). Israel continues to feel the wrath of God for her disobedience. "Woe to them that are at ease in Zion ... that drink wine [*yayin*] in bowls ... they are not grieved for the affliction of Joseph" (Amos 6:1,6). Wine is used here as an illustration of forgetting the most important matters.

Habakkuk

"Woe unto him that giveth his neighbour drink, that puttest thy bottle to him, and makest him drunken..." (Hab. 2:15). "Because he transgresseth by wine [*yayin*—fermented], he is a proud man...who enlargeth his desire as hell" (Hab. 2:5).

Hosea

"...The children of Israel, who look to other gods, and love flagons of wine [*enab*—to bear fruit; ripe grape]" (Hosea 3:1). "**Whoredom and wine** [*yayin*—fermented] **and new wine** [*tiyrosh*—expulsion of fresh grape juice; freshly squeezed new sweet wine] **take away the heart**" (Hosea 4:11). "**The princes have made him sick with bottles of wine** [*yayin*]**...they assemble themselves for corn and wine** [*tiyrosh*]**, and they rebel against me**" (Hosea 7:5,14). Ephraim, the Bible says, is a drunkard (Isa. 28:1). "**Ephraim is joined to idols: let him alone**" (Hosea 4:17).

Isaiah

"**How is the faithful city become a harlot...thy wine** [*cobe*—a drink, especially an alcoholic beverage] **mixed with water**" (Isa. 1:21–22). Isaiah portrayed Jerusalem as a city that had been compromised by spiritual dilution. No doubt Jesus recalled this verse when He wept over the demise of the Holy City. "**Woe unto them that rise up early in the morning, that they may follow strong drink** [*shekar*—intoxicant; intensely alcoholic liquor; strong drink]**; that continue until night, till wine** [*yayin*— fermented] **inflame them! And the harp, and the viol, the tabret, and pipe, and wine** [*yayin*]**, are in their feasts: but they regard not the work of the Lord, neither consider the operation of his hands ... Woe unto them that are mighty to drink wine** [*yayin*—fermented]**, and men of strength to mingle strong drink** [*shekar*]**: which justify the wicked for reward, and** take away the righteousness of the righteous from him!" (Isa. 5:11–12, 22–23).

"And behold...eating flesh, and drinking wine [*yayin*—fermented]: **let us eat and drink; for to morrow we shall die**" (Isa. 22:13). "**The new wine** [*tiyrosh*—expulsion of fresh grape juice; freshly squeezed new sweet wine; rarely fermented] **mourneth, the vine languisheth, all the merry-hearted do sigh. The mirth of tabrets ceaseth, the noise of them that rejoice endeth, the joy of the harp ceaseth. They shall not drink wine** [*yayin*]**with a song; strong drink** [*shekar*—intoxicant; intensely alcoholic liquor; strong drink] **shall be bitter to them that drink it**" (Isa. 24:7–9). False days of happiness are over as the judgments of God had now come upon the land and its ungrateful inhabitants. "**There is crying for wine** [*yayin*] **in the streets;...the mirth of the land is gone**" (Isa. 24:11). God notes in prophecy how rampant the use of alcohol was amongst His beloved children.

"**Woe to the crown of pride, to the drunkards of Ephraim, whose glorious beauty is a fading flower...them that are overcome with wine** [*yayin*—fermented]**!...the drunkards of Ephraim, shall be trodden under feet...they also have erred through wine** [*yayin*], **and through strong drink** [*shekar*—intoxicant; intensely alcoholic liquor; strong drink] **are out of the way; the priest and the prophet have erred through strong drink** [*shekar*], **they are swallowed up of wine** [*yayin*], **they are out of the way through strong drink** [*shekar*]**; they err in vision, they stumble in judgment. For all tables are full of vomit and filthiness, so that there is no place clean**" (Isa. 28:1,3,7–8).

"**Therefore hear now this, thou afflicted, and drunken, but not with wine** [*yayin*—fermented]**...Behold, I have taken out of thine hand the cup of trembling, even the dregs of the cup of my fury; thou shalt no more drink it again**" (Isa. 51:21–22). Over again, the Lord rebukes Israel, using their obsession with drinking wine as a spiritual object lesson. "**Yea, they are greedy dogs which can never have enough....Come ye, say they, I will fetch wine** [*yayin*]**, and we will fill ourselves with strong drink** [*shekar*—intoxicant; intensely alcoholic liquor; strong drink]**; and to morrow shall be as this day, and much more abundant**" (Isa. 56:11–12).

Jeremiah

...**Every bottle shall be filled with wine** [*yayin*—fermented]**: and they shall say unto thee, Do we not certainly know that every bottle shall be filled with wine** [*yayin*]**? Thus saith the Lord, Behold, I will fill all the** inhabitants of this land, even the kings that sit upon David's throne, and the priests, and the prophets, and all the inhabitants of Jerusalem, with drunkenness" (Jer. 13:12–13). Drunkenness is viewed as a self-inflicted means of punishment.

"Mine heart within me is broken because of the prophets; all my bones shake; I am like a drunken man, and like a man whom wine [*yayin*—fermented] hath overcome, because of the Lord, and because of the words of His holiness" (Jer. 23:9). Jeremiah, the "weeping prophet," is heartbroken over the influence of false prophets in the land. He uses alcohol to symbolize his broken-hearted, shaken, and defeated condition.

"…Take the wine [*yayin*—fermented] cup of this fury at my hand, and cause all the nations, to whom I send thee, to drink it. And they shall drink, and be moved, and be mad, because of the sword that I will send among them. Then took I the cup at the Lord's hand, and made all the nations to drink, unto whom the Lord had sent me: To wit, Jerusalem, and the cities of Judah, and the kings thereof…to make them a desolation, an astonishment, an hissing and a curse…" (Jer. 25:15–18). The Lord's disgust with this rebellious nation reached the limit in this illustration of drunkenness. Insanity, fury, violence, desolation, mocking, and a curse are couched around the sustained use of alcohol. "Babylon hath been a golden cup in the Lord's hand, that made all the earth drunken: the nations have drunken of her wine [*yayin*]; therefore the nations are mad" (Jer. 51:7).

Joel

"Awake, ye drunkards, and weep; and howl, all ye drinkers of wine [*yayin*—fermented], because of the new wine [*aciyc*—freshly squeezed juice; new, just-trodden sweet wine], for it is cut off from your mouth" (Joel 1:5). "…I shall bring again the captivity of Judah" (Joel 3:1). "…[Ye have] sold a girl for wine [*yayin*], that they might drink" (Joel 3:3].

Micah

"If a man walking in…falsehood do lie, saying, I will prophesy unto thee of wine [*yayin*—fermented] and of strong drink [*shekar*—intoxicant; intensely alcoholic liquor; strong drink]; he shall even be the prophet of this people" (Mic. 2:11). "Thou shalt sow, but thou shalt not reap… sweet wine [*tiyrosh*—expulsion of fresh grape juice; freshly squeezed new sweet wine]…[thou] shalt not drink wine [*yayin*]" (Mic. 6:15).

Moses

Moses relays the pending judgment of God upon a people who were unmindful of this: **"Of the Rock that begat thee thou art unmindful...For their vine is of the vine of Sodom, and of the fields of Gomorrah: their grapes are grapes of gall, their clusters are bitter. Their vine is the poison of dragons, and the cruel venom of asps"** (Deut. 32:18, 32–33).

Zechariah

"...And they shall drink, and make a noise as through wine [*yayin***—fermented]..."** (Zech. 9:15). **"And they of Ephraim shall be like a mighty man, and their heart shall rejoice as through wine [***yayin***]..."** (Zech. 10:7).

John the Revelator

"...If any man worship the beast and his image..., the same shall drink of the wine [*oinos*—wine, literally or figuratively] **of the wrath of God, which is poured out without mixture into the cup of his indignation..."** (Rev. 14:9–10). The *Amplified Version* of the Bible says, **"...the wrath of God, mixed undiluted into the cup of His anger"** (Rev. 14:10, AMP).

"...The great Babylon came in remembrance before God, to give unto her the cup of the wine [*oinos*—wine, literally or figuratively] **of the fierceness of his wrath"** (Rev. 16:19). **"...I will shew unto thee the judgment of the great whore...with whom the kings of the earth have committed fornication, and the inhabitants of the earth have been made drunk with the wine** [*oinos*] **of her fornication"** (Rev. 17:1–2].

"...Babylon the great is fallen is fallen...For all nations have drunk of the wine [*oinos*—wine, literally or figuratively] **of the wrath of her fornication..."** (Rev. 18:2–3; 14:8). **"...Babylon, that mighty city...is thy judgment come...And the merchants of the earth shall weep and mourn over her; for no man buyeth their merchandise any more:...wine** [*oinos*]**... and souls of men"** (Rev. 18:10–11,13).

In the Lord's wisdom, He used fermented spirits over the centuries to hammer home a vital point in the last days. Spiritual Babylon is portrayed as having all the characteristics of a drunken man. In terms every reader of Scripture could understand, wicked Babylon is revealed as being fierce and fornicating. She is drinking pure alcohol, and is under judgment and insane. At last, mighty Babylon falls—only this time it is for good. Woe unto them who drink the polluted wine of Babylon. Then appears one of the most tender appeals in the entire Bible: an Angel sent from God pleads with humanity, **"Come out of her, my people"** (Rev 18:4). We can be so thankful that God does not ridicule, but actually calls those who are deceived in Babylon, but have pure hearts—His people. He judges not upon our knowledge but upon our hearts. Do you have a heart that is right with God? Do you need to set aside the drinking of spirits and come out of Babylon?

Jesus

"Jesus saith unto them, Fill the waterpots with water. And they filled them up to the brim. And He saith unto them, Draw out now, and bear unto the governor of the feast. And they bare it. When the ruler of the feast had tasted the water that was made wine [*oinos*—wine, literally or figuratively]… the governor of the feast called the bridegroom, And saith unto him, Every man at the beginning doth set forth good wine [*oinos*]; and when men have well drunk, then that which is worse: but thou hast kept the good wine [*oinos*] until now" (John 2:7–10).

People believe they have a license to drink alcohol because Jesus sanctioned its use at the wedding feast in Cana. It was the custom of the times for marriage festivities to continue several days. There can be no doubt these men were somewhat inebriated through their continued use of alcoholic spirits. For centuries, men have looked to discredit the Bible by finding contradictions within its writings. Jesus had guided holy men of old as they penned what would later become our Scriptures. It is not credible that Jesus would reverse the counsel of Solomon, who is regarded as the wisest man who ever lived, as well as the multitude of prophets and their stern warnings about alcohol.

A quick Internet search reveals this searing truth: An estimated 6.2 percent of adults over 18—about 15.1 million people—had an alcohol disorder. This included 9.8 million men and 5.3 million women, or 8.4 percent of all adult men and 4.2 percent of all adult women. Is it not foolhardy to assume Jesus created alcohol at the wedding feast, knowing that a certain percentage of the population were destined to become alcoholics after sampling fermented spirits?

Was Jesus immune from condemnation by the holy writers? Did He defy Scripture and supply the village with alcohol so they could continue in their feasting? If the Bible is a sum of its total parts, then it is beyond dispute that Jesus created unfermented wine at the wedding feast. **"Thus saith the Lord, As the new wine** [*tiyrosh*—expulsion of fresh grape juice; freshly squeezed new sweet wine] **is found in the cluster, and one saith, Destroy it not; for a blessing is in it…"** (Isa. 65:8).

If Jesus was of a mind to quote scripture to the ruler of the feast, He could have quoted: **"…Thou didst drink the pure blood of the grape** [*enab*—to bear fruit; grape, ripe grape]**"** (Deut. 32:14). **"…All the best of the wine** [*tiyrosh*—expulsion of fresh grape juice; squeezed new sweet wine] **have I given thee"** (Num. 18:12).

The reason Jesus's wine tasted so good compared to the other wine was because it was pure, unadulterated grape juice. Any child will choose the taste of the juice of the common grape over the dry, bitter taste of fermented grape juice.

"The gift of Christ to the marriage feast was a symbol. The water represented baptism into His death; the wine, the shedding of His blood for the sins of the world…. So abundant is the provision of His grace to blot out the iniquities of men and to renew and sustain the soul."[42]

The gift of Christ to the marriage feast was a symbol. The water represented baptism into His death; the wine, the shedding of His blood for the sins of the world

"I am the true vine, and my Father is the husbandman.... As the branch cannot bear fruit of itself, except it abide in the vine; no more can ye, except ye abide in me. I am the vine, ye are the branches...for without me ye can do nothing" (John 15:1, 4–5). To the disciples, centuries of scriptural illustrations alluding to the vine, the husbandman, and those treading the grapes now made sense. Jesus was always the symbolic vine. To find salvation without Christ would be to embark upon an impossible journey of righteousness by works.

The Passover

Jewish wine-drinking was not part of the original Passover feast given by God to Moses. The Old Testament never mentions using a cup for Passover, only the lamb, unleavened bread, and bitter herbs. The ancient Jews had been instructed to search their houses carefully before eating the Passover supper, to make sure that there was not even a particle of leavened bread in their homes (Exod. 12:19). They had been taught to regard it as a type of sin. Jesus linked leavened bread to sin, warning His disciples of the crafty Pharisees when He said, **"...Beware of the leaven of the Pharisees"** (Matt. 16:11).

Paul wrote, **"Purge out therefore the old leaven, that ye may be a new lump, as ye are unleavened. For even Christ our passover is sacrificed for us: Therefore let us keep the feast, not with old leaven, neither with the leaven of malice and wickedness; but with the unleavened bread of sincerity and truth"** (1 Cor. 5:7–8). *Strong's Concordance*[43] defines *leavening* as *"swelling by fermentation."* Thus, the communion table bread should be unleavened or unfermented.

"All alcoholic beverages contain a certain portion of ethyl alcohol and carbon dioxide. This substance is produced by a variety of yeasts or microscopic fungi acting as a leavening agent on the sugar molecule of fruit juice. They decompose fruit glucose in a process known as alcoholic fermentation."[44]

Fermentation turns juice, or other wholesome products, into dangerous liquor. In the Hebrew language, from which the Old Testament of our Bible is derived, there are multiple words for wine, some of which mean *non-fermented*, while others mean *fermented*. Fermented wine is aptly described: **"Behold, my belly is as wine which hath no vent** [*is not opened*, margin]; **it is ready to burst like new bottles"** (Job 32:19).

During Jesus's ministry, when all Jews were partaking of the traditional Passover feast, He set the stage for Communion in the new Christian dispensation. Immediately after the miracle of the loaves and fishes, Jesus declared to the questioning multitude who were looking for a sign equal to that of the manna from heaven, "**...I am the bread of life...**" (John 6:35). While the Jews mulled over this perceived blasphemy, Jesus followed this by stating, "**...Except ye drink** [the Son of man's] **blood, ye have no life in you. Whoso...drinketh my blood, hath eternal life.... He that drinketh my blood, dwelleth in me, and I in him**" (John 6:53–56).

The stage was now set for the Christian Passover, now known as the Communion service. At the end of the Last Supper, Jesus surprised His disciples. "**And He took the cup, and gave thanks, and gave it to them, saying, "Drink all of it; For this is my blood of the new testament, which is shed for many for the remission of sins**" (Matt. 26:27–28). "**...He took the cup, when he had supped, saying, this cup is the new testament in my blood: this do ye, as oft as ye drink it, in remembrance of me. For as often as ye...drink this cup, ye do shew the Lord's death till he come**" (1 Cor. 11:25–26).

Paul asks, "**The cup of blessing which we bless, is it not the communion of the blood of Christ?**" (1 Cor. 10:16). Symbolically, Christ's blood must be pure because to drink fermented wine would be to drink what Jesus became for us—sin itself. We drink the unfermented grape juice as a symbol of what He was—pure and holy; and Jesus became what we are—impure and unholy. We accept His awesome righteousness in exchange for our terrible sinfulness. Therefore, in the Communion service we should never partake of fermented wine, for it distorts the meaning of the very sacrifice of Jesus. Fermented wine represents Christ being made sin, as presented in the Old Testament sanctuary service. The mystery of Christ being made flesh and bearing our sins in His own body on the tree, while never yielding to temptation, is revealed in the Communion service. Let this service be pure and holy, not an alcoholic mockery.

> *Fermented wine represents Christ being made sin, as presented in the Old Testament sanctuary service*

A term for fermented wine is used twenty-eight times in the New Testament [*oinos*—wine, literally or figuratively] (in Greek), but never in conjunction with the Passover. Yet, even in the church on the sacred

Communion table, Satan's traps are fulfilled whenever fermented alcohol is used during the Communion service. Satan leaves nothing undone to create and foster the desire for fermented intoxicants.

In Israel, wine sales increase by 25% during Passover season.[45] Today, Jews do not restrict themselves from drinking alcohol on their annual Passover feast.[46]

The Nazarene Vow

There is an object lesson given in the book of Jeremiah, concerning the sons of Jonadab and their descendants. There is reason to believe that they partook of the Nazarene vow, or at least the portion of the vow regarding the grape. The Lord used the faithfulness of the descendants of Jonadab, also known as the house of the Rechabites, to illustrate faithful obedience during the toughest of times. Jonadab had commanded his descendants (probably of the tribe of Jethro, Moses's father-in-law) to observe three things:

(1) they should drink no product of the vine
(2) they should never build a house
(3) they should dwell in tents (Jer. 35:6–7).

Clarke's *Commentary on the* Bible[47] discusses these commands of Jeremiah 35:6 in this way:

WINE "Ye shall drink no wine. Ye shall preserve your bodies in temperance, shall use nothing that would deprive you of the exercise of your sober reason at any time; lest in such a time ye should do what might be prejudicial to yourselves, injurious to your neighbor, or dishonorable to your God."

HOUSES "Ye shall not court earthly possessions; ye shall live free from ambition and from envy, that ye may be free from contention and strife."

TENTS "Ye shall imitate your forefathers, Abraham, Isaac, and Jacob, and the rest of the patriarchs, who dwelt in tents, being strangers and pilgrims upon earth, looking for a heavenly country, and being determined to have nothing here that would indispose their minds towards that place of endless rest, or prevent them from passing through temporal things so as not to lose those that are eternal."

Clarke's *Commentary* continues.[48] "The Lord sends Jeremiah to tempt these descendants when they are at their lowest ebb, having been forced by Nebuchadnezzar to take refuge in the ruined city of Jerusalem." **"Go unto the house of the Rechabites...and give them wine [*yayin*—fermented] to drink....But they said, We will drink no wine [*yayin*]...for our father commanded us, saying, Ye shall drink no wine [*yayin*], neither ye, nor your sons for ever"** ([Jer. 35:2,6).

"The Lord uses this illustration of faith to rebuke the citizens of Judah who have chosen to disobey their heavenly Father."[49] **"The words of Jonadab...are performed...but ye hearkened not unto Me"** (Jer. 35:14). Then Jeremiah declares unto the faithful Rechabites, **"Because ye have obeyed the commandment of Jonadab your father, and kept all his precepts, and done according unto all that he hath commanded you: Therefore...Jonadab the son of Rechab shall not want [lack] a man to stand before me forever"** (Jer. 35:18–19). "True Christians may be considered as their genuine successors."[50] The life of Jesus comes to light in the story of the sons of Jonadab: **"And Jesus saith unto him, The foxes have holes, and the birds of the air have nests; but the Son of man hath not where to lay His head"** (Matt. 8:20). Men of renown were separated unto God to do a mighty work, and nothing was to stand in their way, not even the comforts of food and possessions.

There is indication that Jesus took the Nazarene vow—not from birth but through the circumstances leading up to His death on the cross. It was prophesied from days of old and Matthew may not have understood the full implications of this prophecy when he wrote, **"And he came and dwelt in a city called Nazareth: that it might be fulfilled which was spoken by the prophets, He shall be called a Nazarene"** (Matt. 2:23).

To take a Nazarene vow was to take a vow of separation unto God. The disciples could not come to grips with the imminent first death of Jesus. How could they understand Jesus's separation from His Father during the eternal second death experience that He was about to suffer?

The complex Nazarene vow included two distinct characteristics: (1) **"He shall separate himself from wine [*yayin*—fermented] and strong drink [*shekar*—intoxicant; intensely alcoholic liquor; strong drink]...nor eat moist grapes [*enab*—to bear fruit; grape, the ripe grape], or dried."** (2) **"All the days of the vow of his separation there shall no razor come upon his head...he shall be holy, and shall let the locks of the hair of his head grow"** (Num. 6:3, 5).

Three notables were prophesied Nazarites. Two are strong types of Christ; the other introduced Jesus to the world. (1) Of the strong deliverer, who would die to save his people, it is written, **"...The child shall be a Nazarite to God from the womb to the day of his death...his name Samson"** (Judges 13:7, 24).... (2) Of the godly priest who would guide the nation of Israel through critical times, it is written, **"I will give him unto the Lord all the days of his life, and there shall no razor come upon his head...his name Samuel...as long as he liveth he shall be lent to the Lord"** (1 Sam.:11, 20, 28). (3) Of John the Baptist, it is written, **"For he shall be great in the sight of the Lord, and shall drink neither wine** [*oinos*—wine, literally or figuratively] **nor strong drink"** (Luke 1:15). **"The next day John seeth Jesus coming unto him, and saith, Behold the Lamb of God, which taketh away the sin of the world** (John 1:29). "John the Baptist was a reformer. To him was committed a great work for the people of his time.... All his habits were carefully regulated, even from his birth. The angel Gabriel was sent from heaven to instruct the parents of John in the principles of health reform. He 'shall drink neither wine nor strong drink,' said the heavenly messenger."[51] John went forth to prepare the way of the Lord, a voice crying in the wilderness. He was a noble "representative of those living in the last days, to whom God has entrusted sacred truths to present before the people, to prepare the way for the second appearing of Christ. And the same principles of temperance which John practiced should be observed by those who in our day are to warn the world of the coming of the Son of man."[52] At the Last Supper, Messiah chooses to partake of the ancient Nazarene vow, which had always pointed forth to the Christ. Centuries of mystery were swept away. **"...Take this, and divide it among yourselves: For I say unto you, I will not drink of the fruit of the vine, until the kingdom of God shall come"** (Luke 22:17–18). **"But I say unto you, I will not drink henceforth of this fruit of the vine, until that day when I drink it new with you in My Father's kingdom"** (Matt. 26:29). The time of Christ's separation was at hand. His promise to never partake of the pure grape until we are reunited with Him in heaven proves this vow of separation lingers—Jesus remains separated from His beloved brethren.

In Gethsemane, the disciples were separated from Jesus when He most needed their support. **"What, could ye not watch with Me one hour?...He came and found them asleep again"** (Matt. 26:40, 43). "As Christ felt His unity with the Father being broken, He feared that in His human nature He would be unable to endure the coming conflict with the powers of darkness.... With the issues of the conflict before Him, Christ's soul was filled with dread of separation from God."[53] "In His agony He clings to the cold ground, as if to prevent Himself from being drawn farther from God."[54] "The cypress and palm trees were the silent witnesses of His anguish. From their leafy branches dropped heavy dew upon His stricken form, as if nature wept over its Author wrestling alone with the powers of darkness."[55] "Hitherto He had been an intercessor for others; now He longed to have an intercessor for Himself."[56]

Upon the cross came the ultimate separation between the Father and the Son. "He, the Sin Bearer, endures the wrath of divine justice, and for thy sake becomes sin itself."[57] Then **"Jesus cried with a loud voice, saying...My God, My God, why hast thou forsaken Me?"** (Matt. 27:46). The prophet Isaiah foresaw this event: **"For a small moment I have forsaken Thee"** (Isa. 54:7).

"The Saviour could not see through the portals of the tomb. Hope did not present to Him His coming forth from the grave a conqueror, or tell Him of the Father's acceptance of the sacrifice. He feared that sin was so offensive to God that Their separation was to be eternal."[58] "And in that dreadful hour, Christ was not to be comforted with the Father's presence"[59] **"I have trodden the winepress alone; and of the people there was none with Me..."** (Isa. 63:3).

"The sun refused to look upon the awful scene. Complete darkness, like a funeral pall, enveloped the cross.... In that thick darkness, God's presence was hidden."[60].... "In the thick darkness, God veiled the last human agony of His Son."[61] **"They gave him vinegar to drink mingled with gall: and when he had tasted thereof, he would not drink"** (Matt. 27:34). **"And they gave him to drink wine** [*oinos*—wine, literally or figuratively] **mingled with myrrh: but he received it not"** (Mark 15:23).

According to *Strong's*,[62] vinegar was *sour wine*. Inebriating drinks were mercifully given to condemned criminals, to render them less sensible of the torture they endured while dying. This is what was offered to our Lord; but he refused it, in accordance with the Nazarene vow: **"...Drink no vinegar of wine** [*yayin*—fermented]**"** (Num. 6:3). It was also in accordance with this verse in Proverbs: **"...It is not for kings to drink wine** [*yayin*]**"** (Prov. 31:4).

As Christians living in these last days, should it not be our duty to symbolically separate ourselves unto God, to be peculiar as compared to the world? Alcohol is a way of life for lovers of the world. Should we even touch this fermented beverage to our lips? Our Lord refused to take this pain killer. Should we alter our perception of reality? Do we need to resort to spirits to deaden the pain of living? Is the sacrifice of Jesus not enough to have us carry on in faith?

Those churches who continue to partake of the fermented wine in their services fulfill the words of the prophet: **"But ye gave Nazarites wine [***yayin***—fermented] to drink; and commanded the prophets, saying, Prophesy not"** (Amos 2:12).

Christ's sacrifice is panoramic across the globe. **"...These were redeemed from among men, being the firstfruits [***aparche***—a product of the earth in its natural state (unfermented)] unto God and to the Lamb"** (Rev. 14:4). **"But now is Christ is risen from the dead, and become the firstfruits [***aparche***] of them that slept"** (1 Cor. 15:20). At the end of time, there will be two sickles, conducting two different kinds of work.

"And I looked, and behold a white cloud, and upon the cloud one sat like unto the Son of man, having on his head a golden crown, and in his hand a sharp sickle. And another angel came out of the temple, crying with a loud voice to him that sat on the cloud, Thrust in Thy sickle, and reap: for the time is come for thee to reap; for the harvest of the earth is ripe. And he that sat on the cloud thrust in his sickle on the earth; and the earth was reaped" (Rev. 14:14–16). This symbolizes all believers in Christ and the harvest that Jesus spoke of.

"And another angel came out of the temple which is in heaven, he also having a sharp sickle. And another angel came out from the altar, which had power over fire; and cried with a loud cry to him that had the sharp sickle, saying, Thrust in thy sharp sickle, and gather the clusters of the vine of the earth; for her grapes are fully ripe. And the angel thrust in his sickle into the earth, and gathered the vine of the earth, and cast it into the great winepress of the wrath of God. And the winepress was trodden without the city, and blood came out of the winepress, even unto the horse bridles, by the space of a thousand and six hundred furlongs" (Rev. 14:17–20).

This symbolism speaks of the end of time when wickedness has peaked in nonbelievers who will now have to deal with this angel of fire. The slaughter is great, and what better way to describe it other than through the familiar Hebrew winepress.

New Hearts

After the Babylonian captivity, Jeremiah wrote these words to those remaining: **"For the Lord hath redeemed Jacob, and ransomed him from the hand of him that was stronger than he. Therefore they shall come and sing in the height of Zion, and shall flow together to the goodness of the Lord, for wheat, and for wine** [*tiyrosh*—expulsion of fresh grape juice; freshly squeezed new sweet wine]**… and their soul shall be as a watered garden; and they shall not sorrow any more at all"** (Jer. 31:11–12).

"…Gather ye wine [*yayin*—fermented]**, and summer fruits, and oil, and put them in your vessels…and [they] gathered wine** [*tiyrosh*—expulsion of fresh grape juice; freshly squeezed new sweet wine] **…very much"** (Jer. 40:10, 12). **"…They shall build the waste cities, …plant vineyards, and drink the wine** [*tiyrosh*] **thereof"** (Amos 9:14). A priority after the desolation was to restore the pure fruits of the vine. **"In that day sing ye unto her, A vineyard of red wine** [*chemer*—wine as fermenting; pure, red wine]**. I the Lord do keep it; I will water it every moment: lest any hurt it, I will keep it night and day"** (Isa. 27:2–3). God's idea of keeping a vineyard in this day of rejoicing was far different than the Israelite Old Covenant understanding.

"For how great is his goodness, and how great is his beauty! Corn shall make the young men cheerful, and new wine [*tiyrosh*—expulsion of fresh grape juice; freshly squeezed new sweet wine; rarely fermented] **the maids"** (Zech. 9:17). **"They** [children and sucklings] **say to their mothers, Where is corn and wine** [*tiyrosh*]**?"** (Lam. 2:12). Every decent mother teaches her child to desire and strive for purity. **"For** [the unfaithful wife] **did not know that I gave her corn and wine** [*tiyrosh*]**…Therefore I will return, and take away…my wine** [*tiyrosh*] **in the season thereof…"** (Hosea 2:8–9).

The unfaithful bride of the Old Covenant was given everything, as symbolized in the pure blood of Christ, but rejected it. Messiah was soon appearing; would the results be different this time?

"**Ho, every one that thirsteth, come ye…buy wine** [*tiyrosh*—expulsion of fresh grape juice; freshly squeezed new sweet wine; rarely fermented] **without money**" (Isa. 55:1). The prophesied day had come. The Righteous One walked among men; many would thirst for the Word of God, the True Vine; and Old Covenant ignorance would no longer be winked at, "**This shall be the covenant that I will make with the house of Israel; …I will…write it in their hearts; and will be their God, and they shall be my people**" (Jer. 31:33).

Jesus came to change the Old Covenant manner of thinking: …**Moses because of the hardness of your hearts suffered you…but from the beginning it was not so**" (Matt. 19:8). Jesus declared, "**Take heed to yourselves, lest at any time your hearts be overcharged with…drunkenness…so that day come upon you unawares.**" (Luke 21:34).

How widespread was the consumption of alcohol and drunkenness in New Testament times? So much so that this report was given during the events at Pentecost: "**Others mocking said, These men are full of new wine** [*gleukos*—sweet juice pressed from the grape; sweet wine]" (Acts 2:13). During the time of the early rain, Christian character reformation was at full throttle. The apostles denounced the use of fermented wine that was so freely consumed by their forefathers. New Covenant believers, full of faith, with hearts of flesh, were urged to choose holy living over the former ways. God speaks to New Covenant Christians today, likening us to those who are set apart to do His will: "**But ye are a chosen generation, a royal priesthood, an holy nation, a peculiar people; that ye should shew forth the praises of him who hath called you out of darkness into his marvelous light**" (1 Peter 2:9). Christians today are part of the royal priesthood who were forbidden to drink alcohol. Any person who chooses not to drink alcohol automatically falls under the category of being very peculiar in today's society.

> *Christians today are part of the royal priesthood who were forbidden to drink alcohol*

Church Members

"**And be not drunk with wine** [*oinos*—wine, literally or figuratively], **wherein is excess; but be filled with the Spirit…making melody in your heart to the Lord**" (Eph. 5:18,19). Whenever alcohol is involved, it tends to excess. There is only one melody the Lord wants to hear, and it is not one of drunken singers.

"**It is good neither to…drink wine** [*oinos*—wine, literally or figuratively], **nor anything whereby thy brother stumbleth, or is offended, or is made weak**" (Rom. 14:21). Remember this counsel during social meetings. Your drinking could be a very selfish thing if it leads another into a lifetime of woe. "**A bishop then must be blameless, …sober, of good behavior, … not given to wine** [*paroinos*—given to wine; drunken]**.…**" (1Tim. 3: 2, 3).

This same advice is repeated in Titus 1:7. **"The aged women likewise, that they be in behaviour as becometh holiness, ...not given to much wine [*oinos*]..."** (Titus 2:3). Lest we think aged women should be allowed to drink in moderation, the Amplified Bible has a better translation of this verse; it says, **"nor addicted to much wine"** (Titus 2:3, AMP).

"For the grace of God that bringeth salvation hath appeared to all men, teaching us that, denying ungodliness and worldly lusts, we should live soberly...in this present world" (Titus 2:11–12). **"That the aged men be sober...the aged women likewise...that they may teach the young women to be sober...Young men likewise exhort to be sober minded"** [Titus 2:2–6). That Paul would have to exhort young and old, male and female, to be sober shows what a problem alcohol had been among God's people. **"Let us walk honestly, as in the day; not in rioting and drunkenness..."** (Rom. 13:13).

"Wherefore gird up the loins of your mind, be sober, ...at the revelation of Jesus Christ" (1 Peter 1:13). New Covenant believers have the power of Christ to overcome Old Covenant ways of living. **"Be sober...because your adversary the devil, as a roaring lion, walketh about, seeking whom he may devour"** (1 Peter 5:8). The many pitfalls of not being sober are very clearly presented in Scripture. Alcohol was, is, and will always be, the ultimate tool of Satan to destroy men's lives for eternity. **"But the end of all things is at hand: be ye therefore sober..."** (1 Peter 4: 7). No person can stand in the last days unless he or she stands alcohol-free, with clarity of mind, so as to be able to withstand the final onslaughts of Satan.

What kind of company does the drunkard keep? **"But now I have written unto you not to keep company, if any man that is called a brother be fornicator, or covetous, or an idolater, or a railer, or a drunkard..."** (1 Cor. 5:11). **"Know ye not that the unrighteous shall not inherit the kingdom of God? Be not deceived: neither fornicators, nor idolaters, nor adulterers, nor effeminate, nor abusers of themselves with mankind, Nor thieves, nor covetous, nor drunkards, nor revilers, nor extortioners, shall inherit the kingdom of God"** (1 Cor. 6:9–10). Nonbelievers won't be practicing traits in heaven such as **"...witchcraft, hatred, ...wrath, ...heresies, ...murders, ...drunkenness, and such like"** (Gal. 5:20–21).

> *Alcohol was, is, and will always be, the ultimate tool of Satan to destroy men's lives for eternity*

In the midst of the incredibly low standards of Old Covenant living, we discover an anomaly in Moses's day which typifies the modern Christian experience: **"I have led you forty years in the wilderness...neither have ye drunk wine** [*yayin*—fermented] **or strong drink** [*shekar*—intoxicant; intensely alcoholic liquor; strong drink]**: that ye might know that I am the Lord your God"** (Deut. 29:5–6). Are we not a type of the children of Israel, wandering through this wilderness of worldly sin on our way to the heavenly Promised Land? If we want to be led by God and know Him, we too should be abstainers.

The World

"For the time past of our life may suffice us to have wrought the will of the Gentiles, when we walked in...excess of wine..." (1 Peter 4:3). While many Christians defend alcohol use in moderation as being the acceptable norm, let us examine how the non-Christian world has come to view alcohol consumption. Alcohol is a recognized addiction and a sorry temptation. Society drinks to forget, to empower, to gain confidence, or to alter reality. Christians walk as **"...a peculiar people..."** (1 Peter 2:9), amidst the drunks, all the while beholding the greatest folly ever known to mankind—the multiplied curses of alcohol.

"I am not a drunkard," one says, "for I practice moderation and temperance with my drinking. I am a social drinker only." Why not attend a meeting of Alcoholics Anonymous (AA)? Every single soul in these meetings was once like you, a social drinker. AA considers alcoholism to be a disease that afflicts certain people. The Bible also links it to sin, and that calls for overcoming. The AA determines correctly that every alcoholic is formed from his first drink onward and that, in the end, "one drink is too many, and a thousand is not enough."[63] Their motto: *"Nothing is so bad a drink won't make it make it worse."*[64] Members of AA forever say, "My name is .... and I **AM** an alcoholic."[65] Those who are born again into the fraternity of Christ can triumphantly say, "My name is...and I **WAS** an alcoholic."

Alcohol has been the biggest curse and tool of Satan since creation. Satan draws you in slowly. The thief says, "Give me your money or your life." The liquor seller says, "Give me your money AND your life." If the church won't do anything about the use of alcohol, then let the world rebuke you. They know too well the woes of 6,000 years of alcohol.

We live in an age where temperance is defined on billboards that proclaim, "Don't drink and drive."[66] Noble are deemed those who take a cab when drunk or hire a designated driver, while the remainder of the partygoers suffer inebriation. This is known as "drinking responsibly."[67]

In the 1920s, many Temperance Societies[68] brought much pressure to bear on the American government to ban alcohol. Such was man's unquenchable thirst for spirits that criminal bootleggers ruled and the parties raged. Governments took stock of lost taxes and quickly restored liquor as legal trade, regardless of the social cost. The following quotes were penned prior to abolition, showing what sensible people in the world once thought of booze.

"In Chicago the estimate is, one baker for every four hundred and seventy families, one grocer for every eighty-nine families, and one liquor saloon for every thirty-five families."[69]

Dr. Andrew Clarke, physician to Queen Victoria, said, "I am so horrified at the intemperance [consumption of alcohol] that sometimes I feel like giving up everything and going forth on a holy crusade, preaching to all men, 'Beware of the enemy of the race.'"[70]

"Thanks to our brewers and publicans, and the cooperation of the magistrates who license them, and the consent of the Christian church which permits liquor traffic to continue, we have:

1,000,000 paupers…through drink;

100,000 criminals in jail through drink;

60,000 deaths annually through drink;

50,000 lunatics in asylums through drink;

and a standing army of confirmed drunks."[71]

"Nine-tenths of the crime of England can be traced to drink."[72]

"It is estimated that for every missionary who goes to Africa, seventy-five thousand gallons of liquor are sent to that country."[73]

"The tax on brandy forms the most important item in the revenue of Russia."[74]

"Drunkenness is the beginning and ending of life in the great French industrial centers…. It is estimated that at Lille, twenty-five out of every one hundred men, and twelve out of every one hundred women, are confirmed drunkards."[75]

"Mr. Labaree, a missionary in Persia, writes: If I had any sentiments favorable to the use of wine when I left America, my observations during the seven years I have resided in this paradise of vineyards have convinced me that the principle of total abstinence is the only safeguard against the great social and religious evils that flow from the practice of wine-drinking.... There is scarcely a community to be found where the blighting influences of intemperance are not seen in families distressed and ruined, property squandered, character destroyed, and lives lost."[76]

"While it is true that great good has been accomplished by thousands of noble workers in the ranks of the National Woman's Christian Temperance Union..., and other organizations laboring to protect the innocent and uplift the fallen; ...much remains to be accomplished. The most direct and deadly blow that can be given this monster evil is to PROHIBIT instead of *license* its existence."[77]

"Notwithstanding thousands of years of experience and progress, the same dark blot which stained the first pages of history remains to disfigure our modern civilization. Drunkenness, with all its woes, is found everywhere we go.... Considering only the financial aspect of this question, what folly it is to tolerate a business that is making paupers by the thousand! The laws of the land legalize the trade of making drunkards, and then at great expense provide institutions for converting them again into sober men! Can our legislators furnish no better solution of the liquor question?...Let laws be enacted and rigidly enforced prohibiting the sale and use of ardent spirits as a beverage."[78] Only men of strict temperance and integrity should be admitted to our legislative halls, or chosen to preside in our courts of justice."[79]

"[Alcohol] is the mortal enemy of peace and order.... [It is] the demon that has dug more graves and sent more souls unshriven [with unconfessed sins] to judgment than all the pestilences that have wasted life since God sent the plagues to Egypt, and all the wars since Joshua stood before Jericho."[80]

"Alcoholic liquors...are poisonous, increasing greatly the liability to fatal termination of diseases, weakening and deranging the intellect, polluting the affections, hardening the heart, and corrupting the morals.... [Alcohol is] a disturber and destroyer of peace...thus removing the sure foundation for good government, national prosperity and welfare.... [It counteracts] the efficacy of religious efforts..., promoting crime and pauperism, paralyzing thrift and industry, corrupting politics...and the execution of laws."[81]

The per capital consumption of alcoholic beverages in the United States has varied widely. Before 1850, per capita consumption was 6 to 7 gallons annually of pure alcohol per adult. The most radical attempt by the government to influence drinking in the United States came in the years 1920 to 1933, when the 18th Amendment to the U.S. Constitution brought about Prohibition by banning the manufacture and sale of alcoholic beverages.[82] Immediately after Prohibition ended, the consumption shot right back up and, if anything, is higher today. Prohibition's days are over. What is the Christian to do? The world looks to the church for guidance.

The liquor interest is a power in the world. It has on its side the combined strength of money, habit, and appetite. Men whose money has been made in liquor traffic are members of churches, in good and regular standing. They give liberally to the popular charities. But above the tribunal of the church is the tribunal of God. The money of the liquor dealer is stained with blood, and a curse rests upon it. The world and the church may have approval for the man who has gained wealth by degrading the human soul, but the William Shakespeare writes, "O that men should put an enemy in their mouths to steal away their brains!"[83]

U.S. President William McKinley said, "The liquor traffic is the most degrading and ruinous of all human pursuits."[84]

The Alcohol Poem

Look not upon the wine
That sparkles in its flow,
For death is slumbering there,
Beneath its ruddy glow.
No happiness it bringeth,
At last it only stingeth;
It biteth, and it wringeth,
The heart with bitter woe.

Lift up the tempted soul
Now fallen in despair,
Direct his thoughts above,
To God, who heareth prayer.
His arm in mighty power
Can bid the demon cower,
And in temptation's hour
Will prepare an escape.

F.E. Belden [85]

Liquor Sellers

"Woe to him that buildeth a town with blood, and stablisheth a city by iniquity!" (Hab. 2:12). "Many, who would hesitate to place liquor to a neighbor's lips, will engage in the raising of hops…,"[86] grains, and grapes destined to the distillery. In the light of the law of God, Christians cannot conscientiously engage in the manufacture of spirits for the marketplace. The business of manufacturing and selling alcohol is robbery. Every dollar they add to their gain has brought a curse to the spender. "It is through the greed of gain and the lust of appetite that the grains and fruits given for our sustenance are converted into poisons that bring misery and ruin."[87] "… The liquor seller deals out to his victims that which corrupts and destroys mind and body…. Like the mystic Babylon of the Apocalypse, he is dealing in 'slaves.'"[88] "Fathers and husbands and brothers, the stay and hope and pride of the nation, are steadily passing into the liquor dealer's haunts, to be sent back wrecked and ruined…. In many a household, little children, even in the innocence and helplessness of babyhood, are in daily peril through the neglect, the abuse, and vileness of drunken mothers…. Even among the heathen, men of intelligence recognize and protest against [alcohol] as a deadly poison…. The ungoverned passions of the savage, stimulated by drink, drag him down to degradation before unknown…, proving the destruction of whole tribes and races.[89]

"Behind the liquor seller stands the mighty destroyer of souls, and every art which earth or hell can devise is employed to draw human beings under his power."[90] "To license the liquor traffic is to legalize and foster it. It cannot exist nor thrive without the patronage of each rising generation, a large number of whom it must necessarily ruin, body, soul, and spirit. For the state to receive money from such a source… [is] highly reprehensible."[91]

Make no mistake about it, Satan's snare purposes the youth to enter enchanted ground. Prestige, confidence, adulthood, and the opportunity for relaxed morals are presented in glowing terms throughout the media. Friends are enlisted as the devil's enticers, cleverly deployed to increase alcohol's dependent ranks. Governments who once shunned alcoholic beverages for the well-being of their citizenry now encourage its widespread use, counting upon liquor continuance to solidify the tax base. Liquor manufacturers sponsor the most charitable organizations and sporting events, rising to prominence as society's most outstanding citizens.

Temperance

"The fruit of the Spirit is...temperance....Add to your faith... temperance....Every man that striveth for the mastery is temperate in all things" (Gal. 5:22,23; 2 Peter 1:5–6; 1 Cor. 9:25). All intoxicating drinks are deceptive. They seem to promote happiness, but cause the greatest unhappiness and misery. To intemperance may be attributed much of the world's sorrow. Temperance Societies, once a harbinger against alcohol's ruin of society, are a distant memory. To find an abstainer, one looks to the Christian church for hope. Even the conservative Amish drink brandy, and the Hutterites are busy making wine. Many Christians see nothing wrong with drinking in moderation.

> *Temperance Societies, once a harbinger against alcohol's ruin of society, are a distant memory. To find an abstainer, one looks to the Christian church for hope*

"One of the subtlest effects of this many-sided drug is to produce a craving for itself, while weakening the will that could resist that craving."[92] ["All unnatural excitants are harmful, and they cultivate the desire for liquor."[93] "The food is often such as to excite a desire for stimulating drinks. Luxurious dishes are placed before the children—spiced foods, rich gravies, cakes, and pastries. This highly seasoned food irritates the stomach, and causes a craving for still stronger stimulants.... Tobacco weakens the brain, and paralyzes its fine sensibilities. Its use excites a thirst for strong drink, and in very many cases lays the foundation for the liquor habit."[94]

"How can the user of [alcoholic beverages] give to God an undivided heart? It is impossible. Neither can he love his neighbor as himself. The darling indulgence engrosses all his affections...."[95] "When the appetite for spirituous liquor is indulged, the man voluntarily places to his lips the draught which debases below the level of the brute him who was made in the image of God."[96]

"Moderate drinking is the school in which men are receiving an education for the drunkard's career…. Satan keeps the mind in a fever of unrest; and the poor victim, imagining himself perfectly secure, goes on and on, until every barrier is broken down, every principle sacrificed. The strongest resolutions are undermined, and eternal interests are too weak to keep the debased appetite under the control of reason. Some are never really drunk, but are always under the influence of mild intoxicants. They are…not really delirious, but as truly imbalanced; for the nobler powers of the mind are perverted."[97]

"So gradually does Satan lead away from the strongholds of temperance, so insidiously do wine and cider exert their influence upon the taste that the highway to drunkenness is entered upon all unsuspectingly."[98] "It is a hard matter to overcome and chain a full-grown lion."[99]

The saintly Daniel purposed in his heart not to drink the king's portion of wine (Dan. 1:5,8,16). The children sing the song, *Dare to be a Daniel*.[100] Oh, if men would stand up and follow the temperance example set forth by their Lord and his noble men. The world is addicted to pain killers on all sides, with alcohol being chief. However, the true Christian walks in the footsteps of Jesus and believes in His promise, **"My grace is sufficient for thee…"** (2 Cor. 12:9).

Help the Tempted

"No man also having drunk old wine straightway desireth new: for he saith, The old is better" (Luke 5:39). "In dealing with the victims of [alcohol], we must remember that we are not dealing with sane men, but with those who...are under the power of a demon.... Think not of the [person's] repulsive, forbidding appearance, but of the precious life that Christ died to redeem. As the drunkard awakens to a sense of his degradation, do all in your power to show that you are his friend. Speak no word of censure. Let no act or look express reproach or aversion. Very likely the poor soul curses himself. Help him to rise. Speak words that will encourage faith.... Open the Bible before the tempted, struggling one, and over and over again read to him the promises of God. These promises will be to him as the leaves of the tree of life...."[101] You must hold fast to those whom you are trying to help, else victory will never be yours."[102]

"They will be continually tempted to do evil. Again and again they will be almost overcome by the craving for strong drink; again and again they may fall; but do not, because of this, cease your efforts."[103] The last words of King David to Solomon, then a young man and soon to receive the crown of Israel, were **"Be thou strong therefore, and shew thyself a man"** (1 Kings 2:2).

God calls for the self-indulgent "to arouse and in the strength of Christ win back the God-given manhood that has been sacrificed through sinful [intemperance]. Feeling the terrible power of temptation..., many a man cries in despair, 'I cannot resist evil.' Tell him that he can, that he must resist.... His promises and resolutions are like ropes of sand. The knowledge of his broken promises and forfeited pledges weakens his confidence in his own sincerity and causes him to feel that God cannot accept him or work with his efforts. But he need not despair. Those who put their trust in Christ are not to be...held in bondage to the lower nature, they are to rule every appetite and passion."[104]

"The Savior took upon Himself the infirmities of humanity and lived a sinless life, that men might have no fear that because of the weakness of human nature they could not overcome. Christ came to make us 'partakers of the divine nature,' and His life declares that humanity, combined with divinity, does not commit sin."[105] Nothing is apparently more helpless, yet really more invincible, than the soul that feels its nothingness and relies wholly on the merits of the Savior.[106]

Alcohol and Health

"Beloved, I wish above all things that mayest prosper and be in health, even as thy soul prospereth" (3 John 2). "Of all men in the world, the physician and minister should have strictly temperate habits. The welfare of society demands total abstinence of them, for their influence is constantly telling for or against"[107] the improvement of society. Alcoholic beverages cause much more physical disease than any other drug, whether legal or illegal.[108] They are a curse on humanity. "Overall, harmful use of alcohol is responsible for 5.1% of the global burden of disease."[109]

"If thou wilt diligently hearken to the voice of the Lord thy God, and wilt do that which is right in his sight, and wilt give ear to his commandments, and keep all his statutes, I will put none of these diseases upon thee, which I have brought upon the Egyptians: for I am the Lord that healeth

thee" (Exod. 15:26). Alcohol is not a disease coming upon unsuspecting, unfortunate souls. It is a sin. Hearken unto God, and say goodbye to Satan's beverage of choice. Instead, drink in the Water of Life freely so that you never thirst again.

"Do you not know that your body is a temple of the Holy Spirit...so then honor and glorify God with your body" (1 Cor. 6:19–20, AMP).

Let's look at how alcoholic beverages affect different parts of our body temple.

Brain

"Alcohol tends to destroy the higher forms of cells, those directly concerned with the vital processes, particularly the delicate brain-cells, and to replace them with useless and harmful connective tissue, or what is commonly known as scar tissue."[110] Alcohol causes mild to moderate impairment of the intellectual processes.[111] When alcohol is present in the body, there is a decreased in the flow of oxygenated blood to the brain tissue.[112]

Under its influence, people are persuaded easily to do things that are completely contrary to their established ideals. Alcohol alters the functions of the brain; thus qualifies as a drug.[113] The reason a person feels elated under the influence of alcohol is that the intellectual functions of his brain are suppressed. With the usual inhibitions removed, he says and does things that he would ordinarily refrain from. A vicious cycle is established whereby the inadequate or frustrated person drinks more and more in order to keep himself from realizing his supposed personal shortcomings. The use of liquor as a release from unpleasant reality may be more of a temptation to an unsuccessful person than it is to one who feels happy in his accomplishments.[114]

Alcohol anesthetizes the conscience and the brain centers for self-control and inhibition.[115] Alcohol offers a false security of health but in reality it ruins it. Alcohol cannot nourish for it is devoid of proteins, minerals, and vitamins; it actually inhibits the absorption of some vitamins.[116] With increasing concentrations of alcohol in one's body tissues, the early stage of exhilaration gives way to a stage of depression of the vital functions."[117] "Delirium tremens are a complication in which a person may become confused and disorientated sometimes resulting in hallucinations.[118] At least one-half of the fatalities in highway accidents are traceable to someone's use of alcohol.[119]

Bones

"All alcoholic beverages increase uric acid levels in the blood, but beer has the greatest impact…and is contraindicated for those suffering from gout."[120] Bone fracture in women who drink one large glass of wine or more a day is 2.33 times greater risk for hip fracture than those who do not drink.[121]

Cancer

"The General Direction of Health in Portugal conducted a study….It was observed that the greater the wine consumption, the higher the risk of stomach cancer. Those consuming less than one glass per day are at 36% higher risk; one bottle or more a day are at almost four times greater risk than nondrinkers….A study in the United States [involving nearly 90,000 women] showed that those who consumed…about 150 ml of wine are at 2.5 times higher risk of breast cancer than those who do not drink."[122]

Alcohol can be linked to at least seven types of cancer…Those drinking one drink a day had an increased risk of bowel cancer.[123]

There is an increase in cancer susceptibility in those tissues that come into direct contact with the alcohol: the mouth, the pharynx, the larynx, the esophagus, and the stomach."[124]

Circulation

"The vessels of the skin dilate under the influence of alcohol. This accounts for a person's flushed appearance after drinking. It gives him the false impression that he is warm even in cold surroundings. Alcoholic beverages give a warm sensation, but in reality they cool the body by increasing the blood flow near the skin, causing a loss of body heat."[125]

Headaches

"Red wine and beer are the products most responsible for migraine headaches. Alcohol is a chemical called *ethanol*. "Ethanol may cause headaches by several means. First, it is a direct vasodilator which, in some individuals, may cause a headache. Second, ethanol is a natural diuretic; this leads to excretion of salt, vitamins, and minerals from the body through the kidneys. Excess consumption of ethanol may produce dehydration and chemical imbalances in the body. Except in [homemade] "moonshine," we consume ethanol in beverages that contain other chemicals. These chemicals are called *congeners*, which impart the specific tastes and flavors that make each beverage unique. These congeners also have a variety of effects that can cause headaches, alter other chemicals in the body, and induce the hangover effect if consumed in excess."[126]

Heart

The possible beneficial action of red wine on cardiovascular health has been intentionally exaggerated for commercial reasons. Red wine as a prevention for heart disease should not be promoted as a public health measure.[127]

Excessive alcohol consumption increases the progression of atherosclerosis (hardening of the arteries) and increases the risk of a stroke.[128] Regular or high alcohol use can hurt your heart and lead to diseases of the heart muscle (cardiomyopathy. Drinking alcohol regularly can also raise your blood pressure.[129]

Liver

"The liver is the first processing and purifying station for substances that the blood brings from the intestine. Avoid alcoholic beverages. There is a type of liver disease (hepatopathy) caused primarily by the consumption of alcoholic beverages. Alcohol is a true poison for the liver's cells. Regardless of dose, it is highly destructive to the liver, which it degenerates and destroys."[130] When a person drinks heavily, the body starts to replace the liver's healthy tissue with scar tissue. This is alcoholic liver cirrhosis.[131] The liver becomes shrunken and nodular and progressively ceases to function. Other side effects include bleeding from the esophagus, accumulation of fluid in the abdomen.[132]

Lungs

"Alcohol depresses the respiratory functions. A quantity of alcohol sufficient to make a person oblivious to his discomforts will interfere with breathing."[133] "When the amount of alcohol in the body fluids becomes dangerously high, the body's vital functions are impaired. When death occurs, it is from paralysis of the breathing mechanism."[134]

Medications

Alcohol compounds the effects of certain other drugs that may be present in the body. A synergistic or potentiating effect takes place with some sleeping pills, or pain-relieving drugs, causing sudden and otherwise unexplained deaths.[135]

Mixing alcohol with certain medications can cause nausea and vomiting, headaches, drowsiness, fainting, or loss of coordination. It also can put you at risk for internal bleeding, heart problems, and difficulties in breathing. In addition to these dangers, alcohol can make a medication less effective or even useless, or it may make the medication harmful or toxic to your body. Some medicines that you might never have suspected can react with alcohol, including many medications which can be purchased over-the-counter. Even some herbal remedies can have harmful effects when combined with alcohol.

Nerves

"Alcohol is toxic to the neurons. Although, at times, it seems to relieve nervousness, its effect is always harmful to the nervous system in the end."[136] "Alcohol depresses the nervous system. It is not a stimulant as many people suppose."[137]

"Long continued use of alcohol causes peripheral neuritis—an inflammation of the nerves which causes intense suffering."[138]

Reproduction

"Alcoholic beverages increase sexual desire, but diminishes the capacity to perform."[139] Alcohol in larger doses produces sexual impotency. Women who drink alcohol during pregnancy can give birth to babies with fetal alcohol spectrum disorder; these babies can have vision and hearing problems, hyperactivity, poor judgment, learning disabilities, heart defects, kidney abnormalities, deformed extremities, and a small head.[140]

"Pregnant women who drink (two glasses) or more of wine a day have a higher incidence than nondrinkers of premature births, low birth weight babies and immature placentas."[141]

Stomach

"**Use a little wine** [*oinos*—wine, literally or figuratively] **for thy stomach's sake and thine often infirmities**" (1 Tim. 5:23). The media tries to suggest that a drink of alcoholic wine every day is beneficial to the body. Thus, a new generation of wine drinkers is spawned. But truly, if it is help for the body that is desired, the person should look to the unfermented grape juice. God inspired Paul to write counsel that a man's infirmities could be healed. Is it the pure grape or is it the very poor second choice bearing the multiple negative side effects of alcohol? Unfermented grape juice is preferable to non-fermented wine in medicinal properties and healing. Some research studies suggest that red and purple grape juices may provide some of the same heart benefits of red wine, including reducing the risk of blood clots, lowering the level of "bad" cholesterol, and helping maintain a normal blood pressure.[142]

"Alcohol affects the digestive organs. It increases the flow of both saliva and gastric juice. It may cause an inflammation of the lining of the stomach and a congestion of blood in this lining tissue."[143] "The carbonation in beer, together with the irritating effect of alcohol, tend to irritate the lining of the stomach, increasing the rate of alcohol absorption..[144] The result of regular consumption of wine or other alcoholic beverages is a permanent inflammation known as *chronic gastritis*. "Indigestion, slow digestion, gastritis, and gastroduodenal ulcer are common among beer drinkers."[145]

Wounds

"And [the good Samaritan] went to him, and bound up his wounds, pouring in oil and wine..." (Luke 10:34). Finally, a positive use of alcohol has been found! Because of their ethyl alcohol content, all alcoholic beverages act as disinfectants and antiseptics when they are applied externally to wounds and lesions of the skin; this is alcohol's only medicinal property that is lacking undesirable side effects. This external medicinal property of alcoholic beverages has been known for thousands of years.

Summary

"Whether therefore ye eat, or drink, or whatsoever ye do, do all to the glory of God" (1 Cor. 10:31).

Centuries of loving alcoholic beverages, which led to personal depravity and the breakup of chosen Israel, have come to an end. Numerous prophecies couched in wine-talk language were well understood by the backslidden nation. Types of a Savior, being set apart and finally separated from His Father, were symbolized through abstinence vows. Jesus was clearly portrayed as the True Vine. A gradual reformation evolved among God's people who were finally urged to live the sanctified life in the last days—a life without alcohol. Babylon, along with its spiritual wine, is fallen along with those who partake of it. Wine use in the Bible has been a lengthy, painful lesson and has served its purpose well.

Thankfully, God is forming a remnant for these last days. Children of spiritual Israel can march through the desert storms of life, requiring no fermented spirits to sustain them. They are heaven bound! Those who will be translated from off this decaying earth, portrayed as the 144,000, are singing a new song—the song of Moses and the Lamb. It is a song of self-sacrifice and total abstinence from all things harmful. Whatsoever they drink, they do so to the glory of God. They follow the Lamb wherever He goes, knowing that Jesus did not create or sanction alcohol use at the wedding feast. Sobriety is imperative to their clarity of mind and purity of moral standards. They look forward to the day when they will drink the unfermented pure grape juice with their Redeemer at the great banquet feast in heaven. What a glorious day this will be! No more separation, no more sin, no more Satan, and, thankfully, no more alcohol.

Do you wish to be a member of God's remnant army? It is not too late—it is never too late while you have breath—to come to God with all your heart and forsake the multiplied curses of the fermented drink. Once you have determined to put alcohol abuse in your rearview mirror, there are two methods to achieve success. One is evolutionary in nature, by joining valuable clubs, such as Alcoholics Anonymous (AA) or by checking into a rehabilitation facility. The other is to take the creation method, whereby God spoke and it was done. The end result is liberty of mind, body, and soul, along with happy families and the respect God intended for you to have from the beginning. A productive life is beckoning. Forgiveness is yours from above.

"[The Lord] will restore to you the years that the locust hath eaten…" (Joel 2:25).

Bibliography

1. White, Ellen G. *Patriarchs and Prophets*. Washington, DC: Review and Herald Publishing Association, 1890, p. 45.3.
2. Ibid., p. 46.6.
3. Ibid., p. 49.3.
4. Ibid., p. 47.1.
5. Ibid., p. 47.3.
6. Ibid., p. 50.1.
7. White, Ellen G. *Fundamentals of Christian Education*. Nashville, TN: Southern Publishing Association, 1923, p. 207.1
8. White, Ellen G. *Patriarchs and Prophets*. Washington, DC: Review and Herald Publishing Association, 1890, p. 45.3.
9. White, Ellen G. *From Eternity Past*. Mountain View, CA: Pacific Press Publishing Association, 1983, p. 23.1.
10. White, Ellen G. *The Spirit of Prophecy*. Vol. 1. Battle Creek, MI: Seventh-day Adventist Publishing Association, 1870, p. 33.2, 34.1.
11. White, Ellen G. *The Great Controversy*. Mountain View, CA: Pacific Press Publishing Association, 1911, p. 531.2.
12. White, Ellen G. *Patriarchs and Prophets*. Washington, DC: Review and Herald Publishing Association, 1890, p. 53.4.
13. Ibid., p. 53.5.
14. Ibid., p. 55.3.
15. Ibid., p. 56.2.
16. Ibid., p. 57.1.
17. Ibid., p. 57.5.

18. Ibid., p. 58.2.
19. Ibid., p. 60.3.
20. Ibid., p. 61.4.
21. Ibid., p. 61.5.
22. Ibid., p. 62.1.
23. Ibid., p. 66.2.
24. Ibid., p. 62.3.
25. WordReference.com. "Wine." 2019. Accessed November 19, 2019, https://1ref.us/xs.
26. Strong, James. *Strong's Exhaustive Concordance to the Bible*. Peabody, MA: Hendrickson Publishers, Inc., 2009.
27. White, Ellen G. *Patriarchs and Prophets*. Washington, DC: Review and Herald Publishing Association, 1890, p. 107.4.
28. Ibid., p. 108.1.
29. Parsons, Benjamin. *Anti-Bacchus: An Essay on the Evils Connected with the Use of Intoxicating Drinks*. New York, NY: Scofield and Voorhies, 1840, p. 220.
30. Kitto, John. *The Cyclopedia of Biblical Literature*. Volume 2. New York, NY: American Book Exchange, 1880, p. 447.
31. Wakeley, Joseph B. *The American Temperance Cyclopaedia of History, Biography, Anecdote, and Illustration*. New York, NY: National Temperance Society and Publication House, 1875, p. 198.
32. StudyLight.org. "Bible Commentaries. Adam Clarke Commentary: Genesis 40." 2001–2019. Accessed November 19, 2019, https://1ref.us/xt.
33. White, Ellen G. *Patriarchs and Prophets*. Washington, DC: Review and Herald Publishing Association, 1890, p. 157.1.
34. Ibid., p. 159.2.
35. White, Ellen G. *The Desire of Ages*. Mountain View, CA: Pacific Press Publishing Association, 1898, p. 25.2.
36. Smith, Uriah. *Thoughts, Critical and Practical, on the Book of Daniel and the Revelation*. Battle Creek, MI: Review and Herald Publishing Association, 1884, pp. 55–56.
37. Ibid., p. 56.

38. Got Questions: Your Questions. Biblical Answers. "Why did Queen Vashti refuse to appear before Xerxes?" Accessed November 19, 2019, https://1ref.us/xu.
39. White, Ellen G. *The Desire of Ages*. Mountain View, CA: Pacific Press Publishing Association, 1898, p. 221.1.
40. Ibid., p. 221.3.
41. Ibid., p. 221.5.
42. Ibid., 148.4–149.1.
43. Strong, James. *Strong's Exhaustive Concordance to the Bible*. Peabody, MA: Hendrickson Publishers, Inc., 2009.
44. Pamplona-Roger, George D. *Encyclopedia of Foods and Their Healing Power, Volume 1*. Dalton, GA: Home Health Education Services, 2004, p. 376.
45. Shuttleworth, Kate. "Israeli wine 'not your stereotypical New World wines.'" *USA Today*. April 13, 2014. Accessed November 19, 2019, https://1ref.us/xv.
46. Zaklikowski, David. "Passover: Why is it permitted to drink wine on Passover when it is fermented with yeast?" 1993–2019. Accessed September 18, 2019, https://1ref.us/xw.
47. Clarke, Adam. "Jeremiah Chapter 35." *Commentary on the Bible, Volume 4 Isaiah to Malachi*. 1831. New York, NY: J. Emory and B. Waugh for the Methodist Episcopal Church, 1831, p. 348–349.
48. Ibid.
49. Ibid.
50. Ibid.
51. White, Ellen G. *Temperance*. Mountain View, CA: Pacific Press Publishing Association, 1949, p. 90.5.
52. Ibid., p. 91.2.
53. White, Ellen G. *The Desire of Ages*. Mountain View, CA: Pacific Press Publishing Association, 1898, p. 686.5.
54. Ibid., p. 687.2.
55. Ibid., p. 689.3.
56. White, Ellen G. *From Heaven with Love*. Bolinas, CA: Shelter Publications, 1984, p. 458.1.

57. White, Ellen G. *The Desire of Ages*. Mountain View, CA: Pacific Press Publishing Association, 1898, p. 755.1.
58. Ibid., p. 753.2.
59. Ibid., p. 753.4.
60. Ibid., p. 753.3–753.4.
61. Ibid., p. 754.1.
62. Strong, James. *Strong's Exhaustive Concordance to the Bible*. Peabody, MA: Hendrickson Publishers, Inc., 2009.
63. Jaffe, Adi. "Addiction help and advice." All About Addiction. November 21, 2009. Accessed September 19, 2019, https://1ref.us/xx.
64. AA Slogans and Quotes. "Hundreds of AA Slogans and Quotes." Accessed September 19, 2019, https://1ref.us/xy.
65. "Alcoholic Anonymous Meetings." The Alcoholism Guide. 2019. Accessed September 19, 2019, https://1ref.us/xz.
66. Glionna, John M. "Sobering Changes for MAAD." *Los Angeles Times*. January 14, 1996. Accessed September 19, 2019, https://1ref.us/y0.
67. "Responsible drinking," Medline Plus. January 14, 2018. Accessed September 19, 2019, https://1ref.us/y1.
68. "Prohibition." History. June 12, 2019. Accessed September 19, 2019, https://1ref.us/y2.
69. *Bible Readings for the Home Circle*. Battle Creek, MI: Review and Herald Publishing House, 1888, p. 305.
70. *Temperance: A Monthly Journal of the Church Temperance Society*, Volume 1, No. 1. September 1908, p. 358.
71. *Bible Readings for the Home Circle*. Battle Creek, MI: Review and Herald Publishing House, 1888, p. 749.
72. Thompson, Vance. *Drink: A Revised and Enlarged Edition of Drink and be Sober*. New York, NY: E. P. Dutton & Company, 1918, p. 154.
73. Kellogg, John Harvey and Case, Thomas. "Temperance Notes." *Good Health*, Volume 23. No. 1. January 1888. Battle Creek, MI: Good Health Publishing Company, p. 100.
74. Dorchester, Daniel. *The Liquor Problem in All Ages*. New York: NY: Phillips & Hunt, 1884, p. 63.

75. Ibid., p. 565.
76. *Bible Readings for the Home Circle*. Battle Creek, MI: Review and Herald Publishing House, 1888, p. 308.
77. Ibid., p. 309.
78. White, Ellen G., and White, James. *Christian Temperance and Bible Hygiene*. Fort Oglethorpe, GA: TEACH Services, Inc., 2005, p. 29.2, 29.4.
79. Ibid., p. 30.1.
80. *Bible Readings for the Home Circle*. Battle Creek, MI: Review and Herald Publishing House, 1888, p. 751.
81. Mitchell, John. In Eaton, E. L. *Winning the Fight Against Drink*. Cincinnati, OH: Jennings and Graham, 1912.
82. Pickett, E. Deets, and Squires, Fred D. L. *American Prohibition Yearbook: An Encyclopedia Pertaining to the Liquor Traffic*. National Prohibition Press, 1912, pp. 26–27.
83. Shakespeare, William. *The Words of William Shakespeare, Volume 8*. Boston: MA: Munroe, Francis & Parker, 1812, p. 40.
84. Pickett, Deets; Wilson, Clarence; and Smith, Ernest, eds. *The Cyclopedia of Temperance, Prohibition and Public Morals*. New York, NY: The Methodist Book Concern, 1917, p. 365.
85. *Bible Readings for the Home Circle*. Washington, DC: Review & Herald Publishing Association, 1923, pp. 753–754.
86. White, Ellen G. *Temperance*. Mountain View, CA: Pacific Press Publishing Association, 1892, p. 98.1.
87. White, Ellen G. *The Ministry of Healing*. Mountain View, CA: Pacific Press Publishing Association, 1905, p. 337.3.
88. Ibid., pp. 338.1., 338.3.
89. Ibid., pp. 339.2, 339.3, 339.4, 339.5.
90. Ibid., p. 338.3.
91. *Bible Readings for the Home Circle*. Washington, DC: Review & Herald Publishing Association, 1923, p. 756.
92. Williams, Henry S. *Alcohol, How It Affects the Individual, the Community, and the Race*. New York, NY: The Century Co. 1909, p. 48.

93. White, Ellen G. *Christian Temperance and Bible Hygiene*. Fort Oglethorpe, GA: TEACH Services, Inc., 2005, p. 16.2.
94. Ibid., p. 17.2–17.3.
95. Ibid., p. 36.3.
96. White, Ellen G. *Healthful Living*. Fort Oglethorpe, GA: TEACH Services, Inc., 1994, p. 114.1.
97. White, Ellen G. *Christian Temperance and Bible Hygiene*. Fort Oglethorpe, GA: TEACH Services, Inc., 2005, p. 33.1.
98. Ibid., p. 33.1.
99. Ibid., p. 31.1.
100. "Dare to Be a Daniel." (Bliss, Philip P.). Hymns with a Message: An Inspirational Hymn of the Week. March 11, 2018. Accessed September 21, 2019, https://1ref.us/y3.
101. White, Ellen G. *The Ministry of Healing*. Mountain View, CA: Pacific Press Publishing Association, 1905, pp. 172.3–173.1.
102. Ibid., p. 173.2.
103. Ibid., p. 173.2.
104. Ibid., pp. 174.5–175.1.
105. Ibid., p. 180.5.
106. Ibid., p. 182.1.
107. White, Ellen G. *Counsels on Health*. Mountain View, CA: Pacific Press Publishing Association, 1923, p. 322.1.
108. Fitzgerald, Kelly. "Why Alcohol Is the Deadliest Drug." Addiction Center. 2019. Accessed September 22, 2019, https://1ref.us/y4.
109. "Alcohol." World Health Organization. 2019. Accessed September 22, 2019, https://1ref.us/y5.
110. *Bible Readings for the Home Circle*. Washington, DC: Review & Herald Publishing Association, 1914, p. 746.
111. Lautieri, Amanda, ed. American Addiction Centers. "Short and Long Term Mental Effects of Alcohol." July 25, 2019. Accessed, November 19, 2019, https://1ref.us/y6.
112. Tolentino, Neil, et al. HHS Public Access. "Alcohol Effects on Cerebral Blood Flow in Subjects with Low and High Responses

to Alcohol." February 17, 2011. Accessed November 19, 2019, https://1ref.us/y7.

113. "Alcohol (drug)." Wikipedia. 2019. Accessed September 22, 2019, https://1ref.us/y8.

114. United States Department of the Army. Character Guidance Discussion Topics: Duty, Honor, Country. Washington, DC: Department of the Army and the Air Force, 1952, p. 122.

115. UW-Madison Specific Alcohol Beverage Regulations. June 1, 2019. Accessed November 19, 2019, https://1ref.us/y9.

116. USCD Student Health Services. "How Alcohol Affects Nutrition and Endurance." Accessed November 19, 2019, https://1ref.us/ya.

117. Benson, Luther. *Fifteen Years in Hell*. Fairfield, IA: 1st World Library, 2006, p. 41.

118. Wikipedia. "Delirium tremens." October 17, 2019. Accessed November 19, 2019, https://1ref.us/yb.

119. Shryock, Harold, MD. *You and Your Health*, Vol. 1. Mountain View, CA: Pacific Press Publishing Association, 1978, 204, 420.

120. Pamplona-Roger, George D. *Encyclopedia of Foods and Their Healing Power, Volume 1*. Dalton, GA: Home Health Education Services, 2004, pp. 365, 380.

121. Tulla, John. JOFLO Health Reformation Center. May 27, 2015. Accessed November 19, 2019, https://1ref.us/yc.

122. Ibid.

123. Drinkaware.co.uk. "Alcohol and Bowel Cancer. " Accessed November 19, 2019, https://1ref.us/yd.

124. Cancer.net. "Alcohol." October 20, 2017. Accessed November 19, 2019, https://1ref.us/ye.

125. Shryock, Harold, MD. *You and Your Health, Volume 1*. Mountain View, CA: Pacific Press Publishing Association, 1978, 422.

126. Pamplona-Roger, George D. *Encyclopedia of Foods and Their Healing Power, Volume 1*. Dalton, GA: Home Health Education Services, 2004, pp. 365, 380.

127. Corliss, Julie. "Is red wine actually good for you?" Harvard Health Publishing: Harvard Medical School. February 19, 2018. Accessed November 20, 2019, https://1ref.us/yf.

128. Science Daily. "Excessive alcohol consumption increases progression of atherosclerosis, risk of stroke." October 21, 2013. Accessed November 20, 2019, https://1ref.us/yg.

129. WebMD. "Alcohol and Heart Disease." August 7, 2017. Accessed November 20, 2019, https://1ref.us/yh.

130. National Light. "Herbal Remedies for Hepatopathies." July 26, 2018. Accessed November 20, 2019, https://1ref.us/yi.

131. Nall, Rachael. "Alcoholic Liver Cirrhosis." Healthline. January 12, 2016. Accessed November 20, 2019, https://1ref.us/yj.

132. Shryock, Harold, and Hardinge, Mervyn G. *You and Your Health, Volume 1*. Mountain View, CA: Pacific Press Publishing Association, 1978, p. 422.

133. Shryock, Harold, MD. *You and Your Health, Volume 1*. Mountain View, CA: Pacific Press Publishing Association, 1978, 421.

134. Shryock, Harold, MD. *You and Your Health, Volume 3*. Mountain View, CA: Pacific Press Publishing Association, 1978, 253.

135. Shryock, Harold, MD. *You and Your Health, Volume 1*. Mountain View, CA: Pacific Press Publishing Association, 1978, 422.

136. Shryock, Harold, MD. *You and Your Health, Volume 2*. Mountain View, CA: Pacific Press Publishing Association, 1978, 31

137. Shryock, Harold, MD. *You and Your Health, Volume 1*. Mountain View, CA: Pacific Press Publishing Association, 1978, 421.

138. Ibid., 424.

139. Ibid., 422.

140. Healthline. "Fetal Alcohol Syndrome." November 9, 2015. Accessed November 20, 2019, https://1ref.us/yk.

141. Pickett, E. Deets, and Squires, Fred D. L. *American Prohibition Yearbook: An Encyclopedia Pertaining to the Liquor Traffic*. National Prohibition Press, 1912, pp. 26–27.

142. Zeratsky, Katherine. "Nutrition and Healthy Eating: Does grape juice offer the same heart benefits as red wine?" Mayo Clinic. 1998–2019. Accessed November 20, 2019, https://1ref.us/yl.

143. Shryock, Harold, MD. *You and Your Health, Volume 1*. Mountain View, CA: Pacific Press Publishing Association, 1978, 422.

144. O'Connor, Anahad. "The Claim: Mfixing Types of Alcohol Makes You Sick." *The New York Times*. February 7, 2006. Accessed November 20, 2019, https://1ref.us/ym.

145. Pamplona-Roger, George D. *Encyclopedia of Foods and Their Healing Power, Volume 1*. Dalton, GA: Home Health Education Services, 2004, pp. 365, 380.

TEACH Services, Inc.
PUBLISHING

We invite you to view the complete
selection of titles we publish at:
www.TEACHServices.com

We encourage you to write us
with your thoughts about this,
or any other book we publish at:
info@TEACHServices.com

TEACH Services' titles may be purchased in
bulk quantities for educational, fund-raising,
business, or promotional use.
bulksales@TEACHServices.com

Finally, if you are interested in seeing
your own book in print, please contact us at:
publishing@TEACHServices.com

We are happy to review your manuscript at no charge.

www.ingramcontent.com/pod-product-compliance
Lightning Source LLC
Chambersburg PA
CBHW070559160426
43199CB00014B/2549